Katabasis

poems

Paul Juhasz

Katabasis

Cover Image: *Master of the Aeneid Legend: The Descent of Aeneas into Hell*, circa 1530 CE. Wikimedia Commons (public domain).

Book Design: Rowan Kehn

ISBN: 979-8-9868994-9-7

Turning Plow Press

Praise for *Katabasis*

In the poems of *Katabasis*, Paul Juhasz guides us through the dark landscape of a world below, as identified by the Greek roots in his title. "So many poems about healing," Juhasz announces at the outset, "and still I do not feel healed." The poems here ache with both loss and hope, with an understanding this remarkable poet shares with us, that "healing is not linear. The things that heal us must be returned to with a predictable regularity." Paul Juhasz is a traveler. His longest poem here includes seventeen postcards tracing a ten-day drive through the West. Travel these pages with him. Feel the healing in his words.

—David Meischen, author of *Caliche Road Poems*

Juhasz aptly calls the journey a circle, not a recrossed line, and these poems circle back on the same stories, landscapes, themes like a whirlpool or an old spirograph toy, each rotation a chance for re-examination. Juhasz's poems are travelogues of the exterior and dispatches from the interior. Nature poems and postcards sent from mountaintops accompany intense encounters with the loneliness and wisdom of the inner mind. Often, these are the same poem.

—Quinn Carver Johnson, author of *The Perfect Bastard*

Sometimes you sit with Hope—/ cradling it like a newborn,/ knowing the world it will grow into,/ knowing that world has no place for it—/ and think you are four years behind schedule. Paul Juhasz's poems are not running late. *Katabasis* is a collection of trees: many branches of ideas, emotions and memories. Thoughts reach out in synchronous dance then collect at the root, satisfying and sturdy, the myriad ways of blurring time and how that blurring scars the soul. The book captures piercing investigations of the interior of loss, displacement and interrupted lives, a pile of yesterdays, in eloquent, quiet graceful pleas of episodic longing. Juhasz also asks us to not only visit heartache, but his humanity. Our humanity. Yes, there is bruised hope and beauty here, but these poems also ask that we, if we are fully human, are nature, are an element of the ecosphere, not above it or here to colonize and own, but to respect and embrace as fellow passengers. Many of these poems are in conversation with a wide breadth of writers that inform his work, which speaks to the deftness and texture of this book, from the exquisite distillation of moment to the ability to laugh at himself, the poems laughing beside him. From prose poem to free verse to vaulted lyricism to poetic travelogue, Juhasz's circular lyricism to unflinchingly political poems and satire speak truth to power in modes that are gut-wrenching, delicate and not so delicate. Gwendolyn Brooks said a poet's job is to observe. Paul sees more than most of us. And he sees with more than eyes.

—Quraysh Ali Lansana, author of *Ralph Ellison: More Than Invisible* and *Killing the Negative: A Conversation in Art & Verse*

For Danielle.

Still. Always.

"If I knew the way, I would take you home."

"There is a loneliness in this world so great
that you can see it in the slow movement of
a clock's hands."
Charles Bukowski

"Do you believe in an afterlife?"
"I don't believe in this one."
Cormac McCarthy, *Stella Maris*

"I guess it's healing.
I don't know.
It feels like it's burning all the time."
Christopher Murphy

Contents

/kə'tabəsɪs/

A descent into the underworld, or a literary account of such a journey to the land of the dead, constituting a temporary visit followed by an anabasis (ascent).

Introduction

From time immemorial, all of us, to one degree or another, one way or another, at one time or many times, will be called to survive a descent into the darkness of despair. In *Katabasis* (Greek for a journey to the underground), the poet Paul Juhasz pays witness to such a descent as he traces his life from a cruel childhood, a divorce, the resulting separation from his sons, and a suicide attempt, which sets off a long journey to reclaim himself from self-destruction.

Katabasis is divided into five titled sections, in the pages of which you will find short poems, long poems, prose poems, Haiku, aphorisms, jokes and shaggy dog stories, lament, outrage and exultation. You'll journey into the poet's inner life as he travels across America, crosses borders into plains, mountains, caves, valleys, rivers, carnivals and diners, towns and cities. You'll gain insight from the infinite power and beauty of nature. You will meet few people, and those you do meet will be necessary touchstones to refresh a solo pilgrim looking for light. Juhasz has wisely chosen not to tell the story chronologically. (There is no straight line navigating a way out of the internal cave of a dark self.)

The book begins with three epigraphs which, taken together, provide a holistic sense of how pain and healing are experienced. Three and a half pages of Contents follow the epigraphs, the titles of which are an entertainment in themselves. When read as a whole, the titles create an impressionistic poem as a roadmap to the wide variety of ups and downs on the journey to healing. The poet follows the Contents with a poem concerning how he avoids cliches by replacing overused words with words from "some other rippled fold of time" that will give energy and resonance to desired expression—much like the phrase just quoted.

In the first section, the poet, alone now and living a "reduced life...defined by absence," is unsure whether he can find the faith to continue and wonders if it might be better to welcome death "not as a friend, but as an understanding, which is, of course, a kind of friendship." He's inspired to write again when he finds two old photographs inserted into a collection of Galway Kinnell poems. Perhaps "grafting stale fruit onto a feeble sapling in hope" it will make his life useful again.

In section two, the poet is "both weary of and needful for his dissipation" from the echoes of a painful past; he steps out into a pale blue sunset and grudgingly admits that someday he may see the beauty in it. Through the rest of the section, he engages the outside world in the hope he may forget the past and "behave in harmony with the grace…the unassuming acceptance" of what life has to offer. Like other people do.

In section three, the poet finds introspection difficult as the sound of New Year's Eve fireworks in the park across the street are joined by the sound of gunshots on the other side of the park. He is haunted by the malice and cruelty that motivated the terrors of Parkland, Uvalde, Columbine, New Orleans, the malice and cruelty in Ukraine, Palestine, and around the world, even as he acknowledges that the sounds of violence are "simply an unquestioned fact of life." By the end of the section, the poet finds himself "embraced by the solace of insignificance" in the Badlands of Death Valley, and somehow has rid himself from the "past poison" of suicidal thoughts. And he recognizes that he likes to be alone.

In section four, the past poison threatens to invade the poet's thoughts and start the cycle to self-destruction again. "And like a vaccine that needs a booster" he sets off on a return journey west with hope to find a language that will recapture and make permanent his escape from the past. To that end, the poet documents the trip in a series of seventeen postcards that take him back home to Oklahoma. In the final series of poems, he comes to realize he'd felt a paradigm shift in the Lehman caves in New Mexico: "a darkness of complete and total erasure," a reduction of self to call upon when needed. The poet now knows his cycles of descending dark and returning light are innate, and the job is to use mind and consciousness to keep writing his way from dark to light.

The last section is a single poem that illuminates why the poet's journey has to be told.

Katabasis is a poet's witness to the complexities of the pains endured and pleasures savored in the human condition; an odyssey for our time that inspires a range of thought and feeling so all-encompassing that the book rises from the profoundly personal to the universal.

Paul Austin, author of *Mother and Son*

The Susurrus of Repurposed Wind

My friends jokingly point out my poetry has a penchant for certain words. Hank points out I use "susurrus" a lot. Ky expresses amused surprise when a poem of mine does not contain the word "vector," usually (but not always) in connection with what I call "carrion birds."

Of course, they are right; I do use those words a lot, but only because my Thesaurus offers such paltry alternatives. I do not mean "whispering"; I do not mean "trajectory." And any hack, any would-be wordsmith, can call them "vultures."

(In some rippled fold of time, Joseph Conrad nods his approval, rubs his gout-savaged foot and mumbles over pipe-stem, "yes indeed, the *mot juste.*")

(In some other rippled fold of time, a carrion bird vectors, the susurrus of repurposed wind its soundtrack.)

I have also used the word "remurgent" a lot. I have used the metaphor of the butterfly and of the cocoon in too many poems, and made up my word, "remurgent," to capture what I thought those poems were about, confusing a chrysalis for new wings.

So many poems about healing and still I do not feel healed.
The pain of echo is always there.
The hope of shimmer is always there.
Bracketing me.
Making the butterfly/cocoon analogy hollow,
      empty of meaning,
      nothing but the susurrus of repurposed wind.

Just how many times can one restart?

When They Were Not Yet Shadow

Landscape

Standing before a barrenness of endless plain, dwarfed against
looming plinths,
scrap-yard of sun-bleached bone,
picked-clean cattle skulls,
and dry ink pots,
all scoured by the abrasive exfoliation of wind and dust-devil.

It was fulsome and green once, when I stood here, with them, in the
Long-Ago, a land of garden gnomes and gumball machines, before
this mockery of shadow and void. There are no songbirds here. Only
carrion birds vectoring on the parched air above, dreaming their
carrion dreams;

they, the only movement in this landscape other than the twin Gila
monsters marathoning to the horizon and back, a brindled black and
brick grotesque, making mockery of games once played here.

Under a whittled moon of acceptance, there is nothing but to grow
comfortable in this shadowscape, until its barrenness becomes
familiar, gilded in the costume of Home.

What sound to this surrender?
No call to cry out.
There is no one to hear the echo's rebound,
for there is no one here but me.

The Unintended Consequence
of Unnecessary Expedience

On a sixth of August,
island artists filled their
morning with modest
world-forming,

some in *origami*,
others in *ikebana*;
a few, no doubt, painting
sumi-e, or
scribbling *tanka*,

unaware of *Enola*
and her "Little Boy"
slouching their way towards them
like Yeats's rough beast.

We have had to flounder
in their absence ever since,
stuck in needless lack
bound by a cauterized Truth,
by an amputated Beauty,

a pareidolic haunting within
a form forsaking void,
this echo of a time when
they were not yet shadow.

The End of All We Have Known

"I saw the greatest minds of my generation
destroyed by madness"
Allen Ginsberg, "Howl"

It's happening again, Allen.

We now know the how,
and we now know the why.
And because of the red hats,
we also now know the who

(and what may sting most, Allen,
is that after this big reveal,
we can't escape the accusation
we knew all the while, but denied it,
not three times like Peter, but daily,
with the reflexive fear of the child scared
to face the monster under the bed).

But philosophers have long told us
the illumination of one's ignorance,
of one's idealistic naiveté, is both good and necessary.
So it is the other, unformed questions,
the ones we did not know to ask,
whose answers elude us still,
that fuels this next madness.

Maybe not madness but a despair,
a longing to get back to some sense of wholeness
that probably never existed before
and certainly now won't again.

People in Italy and Germany,
in Hungary and Cambodia,
in Venezuela and Chile, tremble for us,
for they know what comes next.

Will the panic attacks ever stop, Allen,
that feeling of drowning on dry land,
of being crushed by some nonspecific

but constant incorporeal weight?
Or will we just get used to them?

For how long are we expected
to breathe in this miasma?
How do we whisper ourselves to sleep
with promises it will all be ok,
knowing tomorrow's dawn calls down
the end of all we have known?

I read somewhere that the albatross can fly
unfathomable distances,
across vast oceans,
without pause;
has the strength to endure unceasing headwinds,
can withstand the vagaries of atmosphere,
survive the excesses of climate.

But just because they *can*
should not suggest they want to.
Surely, they too long for rest,
a place to land and gather oneself.

Where, Allen, in this looming time
of eternal Moloch, can we land now?
And who will be left to record our howls?

Wait A Minute, Mr. Postman

Without the path of connection an address provides,
the completion of a union of which the writer is but half,
a postcard is nothing but a picture someone else took,
a disembodied moment from an experience not yours,
that you can tape to your wall and look at from time to time,
hoping, by proxy, to mortar together fragments of a life.
A world afresh with the shimmer of possibility,
a confined universe you can populate with
whomever you wish, while you whisper into the dark,
"Wish you were here."

Go On Without Me

And would it have been worth it, after all

. . . .

To say: "I am Lazarus, come from the dead,
Come back to tell you all, I shall tell you all"
 T.S. Eliot, "The Love Song of J. Alfred Prufrock"

In the war movies I watched as a kid, I was always unnerved by that one soldier leading the charge, leaping onto coils of barbed wire to press down a path for those behind. He rarely had a name, typically noted in the credits with just a number. On rare occasions when the screenwriter was more metaphysically aware, he was called "Sacrificial Soldier."

He would haunt me long after the credits rolled. The thought of razors slashing his flesh, of metal barbs piercing his body. And to what end? It is the battle—who lost and who won—that is remembered, not some obscure sacrifice forgotten in the gore.

Those terrifying images of martyrdom adorning the churches of my childhood pale in comparison to the gesture of that nameless soldier. Christ only wore the thorns on a crown, safe in the Divine knowledge of how it would all play out.

There is no such knowledge, here at the precipice. No sense that others will ever understand or seek to know what informed that leap. Nor can that soldier come back, Lazarus-like, to offer anything more than these echoed words.

Ghost Town

Perhaps it was the breakfast that did it. A reunion of old friends enjoying eggs and breakfast meat at the Smokestack in the ghost town of Thurber, Texas. Later, as we drive through Stephenville, where both Hank and Michael still work, through shimmered eyes I see my sons everywhere. This is the town square, where I took them trick-or-treating, dressed as Batman and Robin. Down that road five miles is where I once wove the car in between a panicked brace of deer to PJ's amazement. At that hotel, I caught Emerson as he slipped towards the hot tub's concrete edge.

Half a continent away, encased in their cones of silence, do they still believe in a father's love? Understand, marvel, at his protective acts? Or do they unquestion the distance?

I see ghosts everywhere in this town, haunting me with phantom presence like a severed limb.

How do I walk this road hobbled so?

From where do I find the faith they are somewhere up ahead, waiting my arrival?

Aerodynamics

There is something
quite provoking
about a bird that only
hops away from you,

a judgment
that you are not
significant enough
for the flapping
of wings.

A Text Message from a Hypercritical, Emotionally-Unavailable Father Marking the Occasion of the Anniversary of His Estranged Son's Suicide Attempt

I'm glad
you fucked this up,
too.

Long Distance Love Poem

Do you really think a distance matters?
This earth lies 93 million miles from the sun,
yet skin still tingles to its touch.
No. Our distance is nothing.

Nothing more than the pull of an old
postcard from Florence or Santa Cruz,
places painted with words promise-laden;
it is nothing more than the lapping of shore
waves endlessly longing for the new
shapes they create each tide.

Do you really not sense this? I am all around
you still. I am in the ticking and tocking of the wall clock,
and in the telltale susurrus of whispered rainfall.
I am the inner warmth of winter soup, and
the aching of teacups waiting to be filled.

In this lonely, temporary abode,
I place you into my every echo,
place you within every shadow.
Feel it tingle your skin,
and know that this is me?
And that this distance is nothing?

Let it be the warm, whispered breath
in your ear, let it be a slow, soft breeze
dancing across the downy hair along the back of
your neck. Let it be the hand lightly resting
on your hip, waiting on the moment to
turn you into embrace. Let it be this fulfillment
of touch, when the distance between us
becomes nothing.

Fairgrounds

1.

They are taking down the tents, disassembling the rides. Grackles and crows pick over the picked-over grounds, looking for wayward corn kernels, pieces of broken chip, a discarded, foot-crushed French fry. Fair smell will linger for a little while longer, whiffs of street taco, cow shit and communal sweat will whisper the last ten days, of the controlled chaos, the ritual gaudiness across what is now a vacant, tamped-down scar.

2.

Celebrating the harvest in a small suburban community that did no harvesting, we wandered the grounds with a meander we thought was a strut. Surreptitiously drunk over stolen beer (that we never remembered to replace in our fathers' garage fridges in time), pins on our varsity jackets glittering under temporary halogen. Pretending to be too cool to stride through the livestock buildings (why should we, soon-to-be-men, coastal Connecticut men, care about cows and pigs and goats), but striding through all the same. We ate fried dough slathered in marinara; we prowled after girls, a young wolf pack, with only the vaguest notion of what we'd do if we caught some; we rode the Tilt-A-Whirl and rode gunny sacks down a plastic rainbow wave of slide jutted into the night sky, recalling, with a mixture of joy and shame, riding these same with our fathers in the recently discarded years. We feigned an indifference; but also avoided the freshly-abandoned fields once the rides and tents and stalls had moved on.

3.

My son, sharp-eyed cub, sees the neon and flashing bulbs first. New to this Pennsylvania town, we did not know its patterns, its cycles of celebration. We were already running late, but we make the time that must always be made. We played Midway games, liberated a patchwork bear by popping balloons; we ate fried dough (powdered sugar replacing New Haven marinara); we rode rides. He had no interest in the slow, circular ones, unseduced by the sham fantasy of dutifully, rotating police cars or spaceships. He wanted the haphazard jerkiness of The Octopus, with the flashing red and green lights that caught his eye from the road; he wanted the controlled chaos-swirl of the Tilt-A-Whirl. He was too short for these rides, but close enough for carny apathy. I had never heard my son laugh this way before, within the dips and whirls. The bear has long since been lost, but the echo of that laugh lingers. We never had cause to drive by that small miraculous patch of field, tucked behind the volunteer fire department, again, moving on before the next cycle of harvest was complete.

4.

Nothing says you are alone quite like the fair coming to town. The fair is for holding hands, tasting each other's food, sharing the view from atop Oklahoma's giant Ferris wheel, doing the things that win prizes, mass-produced stuffed animals that you win and she keeps or that she wins and you keep (for it matters not which). Centripetal force of Midway rides trying to make your shared oneness literal. Like the grackles and crows, I search for pieces, scraps of sustenance, some seed lost in a blighted field. There has been no harvest for quite some time.

Phantom Kisses

I did not go to work today,
because you appeared in my final dream.
Damp pillow evidence
of the phantom kisses
we shared in the liminal.

And so I turned off the alarm,
curled back under the warm bedsheet,
embraced sleep again in the hope
you would return.

Thanksgiving Haiku

Halftime football lands
Silent on soft frosted grass.
No one to catch it.

Radio Silence

When too many
       songs
remind me of
       you,
there is nothing left
       to do
but stop listening to
       music.

Death Valley Haiku

Mesquite Flats Sand Dunes:
Not one mesquite tree in sight
Not remotely flat.

A Shadow Dreams of Leaves

It is a reduced life I live now, defined by absence. It feels, in many respects, like a waiting room, its corners cobwebbed, the floors speckled with dust and crumb. There is no one to clean for. The magazines have all been read over, the television stuck on one channel of no-interest. There is only one door, and it is not the one I entered by. And there is nothing to do but sit in the cracked faux-leather chair, rustling to find the least uncomfortable position, and wait, hoping someone finally calls my name to enter, knowing they never will, for there is nowhere to go.

Sometimes the room morphs into a fenced yard. Someone whispers the fence is electrified and, shockingly, I don't feel the need to still touch it. Beyond, a tree line decorates the horizon. Fruit trees and evergreens. In this version, I become intimate with the fence line, sleepwalking its circumference each night, dreaming of leaves.

Wordsworth and the Mississippi Kites

"Poetry is the spontaneous overflow of powerful feelings;
it takes it origin from emotion recollected in tranquility."
William Wordsworth, *Lyrical Ballads*

They arrived in late spring. Whether paired or coincidental, I do not know. Adorning the city park across the street with a majesty atavistic and archaic, a grandeur that aches of separation. Surveying the ground below as an afterthought. We are not of their world and never will be.

Fooled by the illusion of permanence, I used to watch them soar through fulsome tree and blithe air, stuck within my own ache of separation, lacking grandeur, lacking majesty, I had thoughts and feelings, of value and of comfort. I did not write those thoughts, those feelings down. I thought I would remember. Trained to hold reflexive confidence in the ability to recall such spontaneous overflow, I thought I would write the poem later.

Now it is later. The birds have left, long ago. Whether paired or coincidental, I will never know. I wish I wrote this poem while they were still here, still soaring. I suppose I am grateful that once I had thoughts of value, feelings of comfort, but I did not attend to them as I should have. I took the soaring for granted.

I was not of their world and never will be.
Wordsworth was wrong:
Nothing real can ever be recalled; it can only be experienced.
And after, there can be no such thing as tranquility.

The Old Men at Walmart

It is not the witching hour, nor anything akin to that, for there is no magic here. Still, there is something solemn about these early Saturday hours; an indifferent gathering, like a storm drain assemblage, when the single old men do their shopping away from the glares and stares, away from the wonderous judgment of community. They wander down their lonely aisles, wondering how it came to this, while silently assembling a paltry pile of items. Barely enough to justify a cart, but pride still keeps them away from the finality of handbaskets. There are no children, begging for candy or toys, at this hour. No wives or partners parsing through future-laden lists and dinner plan promises. There are just the old men.

They do not buy much, for they have lost most of it already. They wander down their lonely aisles, wondering how it came to this, wondering whether they should count out their days in microwave burritos or chicken pot pies. The hardware section nothing but a vague, shadowy echo of days as distant as the Cretaceous, as mythologized as Valhalla. The clothes section sped through, a forced and fated indifference grabbing for shelves (for it no longer matters whether boxers or briefs). Some stay outside, huddled in the lea of the storefront, furtively smoking in passive suicide, but most of us shuffle, fatigued and silent, within; wandering down our lonely aisles, wondering how it came to this.

End of Days

I have my doubts about the necessity of graves. Of what use, these carved voids in earth, to be filled with the need of others, this perfunctory obeisance we pay to traditions as empty as the moldy funeral suit within? Much better to welcome Death as something other than a hole capped with a sterile stone monument. Perhaps not as a friend, but as an understanding, which is, of course, a kind of friendship. What more, at the end of days, could we wish for?

The world seems cold and fragmented, and I, untethered, see no reason to long linger, sleepwalking into an old age, toward this expectation of a geometry in dirt. There is no point in lying underneath a gravestone no one will come to visit. There are far better ways to fill these end of days. Stay five, maybe ten, more years, filling this span with what has long been calling me, landscapes haunted by sons and lovers. Sometimes I will embrace them; sometimes wave them away like morning mist over Crater Lake, like smoldering embers on a Yellowstone hill.

No forgotten nursing home for me, no subterranean rectangle. When the end of days is reached, I think I will just fade away, like Tolkien's elves. Perhaps years from now, readers of my words will wonder what became of me, as they do of Ambrose Bierce. But since Death is a construct for the living, that will be their own affair.

Reading Galway Kinnell's *When One Has Lived a Long Time Alone*

"The future he dreaded seems to have dissolved
on approach, and reassembled behind as the past—
but slightly blurred, being mostly unlived."
Galway Kinnell

Because I have lived this way five years and counting;
Because a friend knew this, and so once lent me her own copy;
Because that one pass through offered a whispered, temporary, balm,
I purchased my own copy at a used bookstore,
hoping to recapture Kinnell's comfort, his consolation of
community,
and there, nestled among the poems, I found two photographs,
mementos from a timeline not my own.

The first, splitting the pages of "The Auction,"
a poem that begins "My wife lies in another dream"
and ends on a shoe defined by the shape of a forgotten foot,
is of an off-centered woman bundled against a snowy landscape.
Before her a red, shaggy, dog gallops in play.
Despite the assumed coldness, her happiness seems beyond
conjecture.

The second, folded into the interstice between sections
unhelpfully labelled "Part III" and "Part IV," is of a man,
flannel-hugged, sitting on a couch. There is the suggestion
of kitchen behind his shoulder. Given his still-fresh
sleepiness and rumpled hair, it seems safe to assume
his mug holds morning coffee. There is just enough blurriness
to the photo to suggest something wrong with my eyes.
He too, it is obvious, is happy.

Are these merely bookmarks?
Or were they meant to mark this book?
And for whom?
Did they take these photos each of the other?
Or is there a third person who once held them both?

I don't want to think the owner is missing these photos.
I want them to be intentional inserts, not missing pieces of a life
desperate for re-collection.

Then again, *I* am now the owner of the photos,
of their imprecise loss. I could cling to their
gossamer thread, like a drowning man
clutching a too-thin twig. I could blend them
into the story of the poems or of my own,
grafting stale fruit onto a feeble sapling in hope
of future nourishment. Or I could replace the book
on its shelf and ponder the import of a life mostly unlived.

Seeds Planted on Mt. Moriah

After Mt. Moriah

The horror of the story is not the thought:
what if the angel did not show up.
The horror of the story is the fact that it did.

What must it have been like,
for Abraham, for Issac,
in all the years after?
How does one recover from
something like that?

For those of us for whom the story hits a bit too close to home,
who have grave, deep-entrenched doubts about the efficacy
        of divinely substituted rams,
who have waited in vain for the perfectly-timed miracle,
who want this parable of parental disregard to do more
        than foreshadow our own alienation,
the Good Book is troublingly silent.
It champions the wrong choice,
and says nothing about the aftermath.

So we can only wonder about Issac?
How it must have felt,
the hand that once lovingly held his
now holding him down with the weight
of a world too casual with its cruelty,
the curved blade of dagger poised and thirsty,
the lust of blind obedience flattening his father's eye;

to glimpse this incontrovertible proof
that different rays illuminate the world,
that the sun was not the sun after all;
how could Issac carry on after such revelation?
What seeds were planted on Mt. Moriah?
And what will they grow into?

And will *he* do the same when the roles are reversed?
If tested by a petty god,
a feebled Abraham now the required sacrifice,
will Isaac stay his hand?

Or will he sacrifice the god
        he can no longer believe in
to satisfy the god
        he can no longer believe in?

Into a Pale Blue Sunset

"if he turned his eyes to look on her,
the gift of her delivery would be lost."
Ovid

He would like to forget. The old Eurydiced days are now but the
spectral blue-black images confined within a negative of a
photograph lost within the shadows behind an empty bookcase
pressed up against the stucco of a mostly barren apartment. They
whisper themselves with the scent of lavender and sage, David Byrne
on the radio, the pages of Joan Didion. Echoes of a happiness
hostaged between the thin aluminum walls of a candy cane cookie
cutter.

The hardest days for him are the ones with a sunset. At one time,
their world was resplendent with them, brilliant and multi-hued. The
kind that made you stop and notice, slow down and savor. She was
always a fan of sunsets. She'd make them cool drinks, draw up chairs
on the balcony, and make him sit and take it all in, the silence of
clasped hands their soundtrack. Their days in the before fulgent with
sunset. He would like to forget.

He finds within the liquid wealth of Dionysus paltry solace,
within the waters of Lethe temporary respite.
He longs for the rending and the tearing of the Maenads, his flesh jig-
sawed into insignificance. He is both weary of and needful for his
dissipation.
He understands that the next time he runs his feet through the
Pacific, she will not be there.
He understands that he will not be permitted to put away the lyre.
He understands he will continue to write poems, but they will be
different poems.

He is both weary of and needful for his dissipation.
He would like to forget.
He wishes he never looked back.
He does not know how to look forward.
He walks out into a pale blue sunset.
He allows that maybe there is beauty in it.
He allows that maybe one day he'll find it.

Pray for Me

That's how Crystal, my twenty-seventh and final
Uber ride of the day, ended her story.

She has three years of probation left.
Then she can "finally" leave Oklahoma.
I don't understand why she would want to leave
this land where I have chosen to settle
       and begin again.
But I also remember the strangling desperation,
the tar-pit-sinking mastodon panic
compelling my flight from the east.

She has three years of probation left.
Then she can see her daughters again.
They are adults now, but haloed
with a patina of hopeful forgiveness.

Pray for me, she asked as she left the car.
I did not have the heart to tell her
I do not do such things anymore,
have no lingering faith in hollow ritual
drowned by its own sham echo-chamber.

So I wrote this poem instead,
which, in many ways,
amounts to the same thing.
She has three years of probation left.
The length of my own unknown and indeterminate.

November Haiku

Reflected forest
at dawn mirrored in fall lake
Only one real, both cold.

Envy

Nature is rife with instruction.
This is hardly a novel insight.
Poets far better than I
have been making it for hundreds of years.

Birds instruct.
Mountains instruct.
Trees instruct.
Every facet of Nature
offers us pedagogy

if we just open our eyes,
unplug our ears,
set free our soul
to wander in wonder.

We can learn from birds
still flying in rainstorm,
model their braggart resilience,
their hardy foolishness.

Or we can envy the beaver in its lodge,
safe within the sturdiness of sticks,
the only entrance though the unbreathable
medium of water.

Shimmer

An oasis off in the close distance,
halfway shy of the horizon,
shimmering.

He knows it is most certainly a mirage,
but he'll stumble toward it anyway,
with the drunken lumbering of exhaustion and thirst
that only the truly lonely know.

Years from now, hearty and well-provisioned
explorers may find his sun-bleached bones
long since forgotten by flesh
among these undulating dunes,
and wonder.

Perhaps they too will know of the shimmering,
but it is unlikely. Few do.
More likely, they will think him foolish and ill-prepared.
They will not hear the sand-scoured echo of his voice,
saying he knew it was most certainly a mirage.

But still, he'll whisper, that shimmering.

And for the short while
he stumbled his way toward it,
he dreamed of water.

Surely that has to count for something.

Hope Is

"Hope" is the thing with feathers-
That perches in the soul.
                         Emily Dickinson

It is not a bird
nor a butterfly
nor anything with wings.
It does not flutter or soar.

Hope is a crab,
shell-armored
against an atmosphere
designed to crush
such frail creatures;

a bottom feeder
surviving on scraps
that float down
through a fractured sunlight.

An Old Man Contemplates Basketball While the Dishes Do Not Wash Themselves

In the cool morning of a late summer whispering of autumn,
I watch a man younger than me (much younger, it seems,
but then again, these days it feels like who isn't?)
shoot baskets in the park across the way.

There was a time I would consider walking over, nod hello,
and begin the communal ritual of rebounding for each other.
The idea ridiculous now, just the taunting chimera of nostalgia.
So instead, I watch from across the street as he makes seven, then
eight, then nine shots in a row.

He is in a zone, oblivious to all distraction.
Focused solely on extending the delight of made basket after made
basket.
While I cannot see his actual expression, I imagine the smile;
grim and determined, surely, but a smile nonetheless.

His streak lengthens to twenty-six before he finally misses,
a clanger that missiles horizontal directly off the court
before rolling to a stop on browning summer grass
dreaming hopeful of fall rain.

I went back inside to the day's meager dishes,
sad to think that if he is anything like me,
it is that missed shot he'll be thinking about the rest of the day.

Unrequited

The carnival was in town three months before anyone noticed. By then, the bearded lady was on a first-name basis with Alice, the cashier at Albertson's; every few days she wandered the aisles, occasionally fingering the razors, dreaming of Barbasol escape. The lion-tamers released their charges with hollow hopes that they would opt to remain, the certainty of a daily raw steak better than shadowy dreams of gazelle (which just goes to show you that lion-tamers only dance on surfaces), while behind their hands, the ride-operators laugh at such foolish religion.

The trapeze artists were all out mailing letters, and the acrobats had long since given up. Those not enfolded into Kansas poems offered only half-hearted exhibitions, barely more than performative calisthenics, in front of an audience of peanut vendors and ride mechanics. The midway barkers found all of this disappointing, but hardly surprising. In a world where everyone wears a top hat, how to tell who from who? Regrettable, certainly, but even the novelty of tractor-pulls cannot compete with monster truck rallies in community coliseums. The jugglers took it hard, though. Assumed the blame, pushed themselves past the mundane predictability of round, tried triangles and progressively harder shapes, stigmatatizing themselves needlessly.

As weeks turned into months and months into years, wind-flapping tents morphed into buildings until it was unclear where the carnival existed and such things ceased to matter.

And the single young child who saw the carnival as it pulled up all those uncountable unrequited years ago was no longer certain of what he saw.

The Age of Heroes

Of what use the hero, if,
after all is said and done,
she says, "but I did not need rescuing"?

If, after the ground is littered
with the vanquished—slain dragons,
heart-staked vampires, giants cut
down to size—she says,
"but they were not monsters at all.
No, none of them were monsters, at all"?

Why risk the wall of thorns,
slashing and hacking one's way to the tower,
should she look down on the debris
and say, "But that was my garden, my view"?

What if she sees all my brave
deeds of derring-do, and says,
"but I did not need rescuing at all.
No, I needed none of these things, at all"?

What if she sees my shield is burnished
and dull, would no longer reflect the gorgon's face?
Knows that in the field of heroics,
there hasn't been a fresh idea in centuries?

What if we've had it wrong all this time?
What if the age of heroes has drawn to a close,
and we, at long last, must now find
another way to be?

The Long Goodbye

They say there is no water
here. A land not barren
but parched. Red cedar
and mesquite, harsh, loveless
trees, soak up whatever is
offered, leaving nothing that
promises a life.

I have tried many times
to leave, only to be lured
back into this valley by
fallow fantasy,
plighting troth to
the frayed edges of a shadowy idea,
a shimmering in the distance
of chimeric possibility.

There are occasionally flowers,
but only after a hard rain,
when the groundsoak is
temporary, filling a fleeting
need. Nothing else will grow,
so there is no reason to stay.
And yet I linger, missing
a life I never had.

So many goodbyes echo
within the valley walls,
bouncing off heartless rock,
making it unclear which
goodbye was the last.

The divining rod is broken,
held together with
strands of abandoned wire and
strips of reused duct tape.

But *surely* there is water
somewhere.

Prufrock's Mermaids

"I have heard the mermaids singing, each to each"
T.S. Eliot, "The Love Song of J. Alfred Prufrock"

I have heard them too, Thomas,
and like your J. Alfred,
they do not sing to me either.

I try to consider things from their perspective,
the mermaids. Their seaweed idyll inviolate, until
the intrusion of middle-aged failure and a self-pity
of sand-strewn solitude,
and find I cannot begrudge them
their detached disregard.

Why sing to those to have lost the luster
of accomplishment?
Why stop the carousel to readmit those
who have jumped off?
They have chosen answers to their questions,
the finality of which
is theirs and theirs
alone.
What business is that of the mermaids?

Leave them their rolled trousers
and their Möbius strip Michaelangelo repetitions
and leave the mermaids
their songs and frolic,
for the sunder is cicatricose irredeemable.

Better, surely, to choose the other way,
the way of the patient etherized upon the table.
In that direction may lie the only bliss
left allowed to us,
much better than beach sand rubbing raw the skin
between toes once hidden within athletic shoes,
sun scalding balding scalps once draped
in wave-like ripples of flowing hair.

The silence of the mermaids is mine as well, Thomas.
Where, then, is the love song for me?
Who will write my poem if not you?
And will I truly drown upon waking?
Or haven't I always been submerged and gasping,
stuck within a leviathan dream
of warm sun, of dry land?

Rinse, Lather, Repeat

In my post-divorce life,
I have discovered the twin joys
of long hair and Paul Mitchell hair-care products.
My favorite is the conditioner
with the promise-laden name
The Detangler.

For decades, spanning teenaged idyll
up through signed paperwork and the new
celebration of finalized anniversary,
my bristled flat-top had no need for conditioning.

But now the glorious Detangler,
cream colored and mucousy
like a stubborn cold,
brings a new luster,
my hair now knot-free and luscious.

It lacks only someone's fingers
running through its silky length,
as awe-stricken as I am
at its full-bodied wonderfulness.

Point of No Return

We never know when our last trip to an amusement park occurs.
It is only in retrospect that we recognize
those moments have passed.
The frightful anticipation of ascent,
the stomach drop of first contact,
the intentional soaking of water rides
and the simple, consistent beauty of carousel horses,
all one day find themselves unaccountably transformed
into silhouette and echo;
we are left with nothing beyond
trying to convince ourselves the new diversions
arriving in their stead are adequate,
paltry and wretched though they are,
paltry and wretched though we know them to be.

Putting Away Childish Things

Why can't we just leave Waldo
         alone
within his longed-for
         anonymity?

Last Man Standing

"We'll go down in history as the first society
that wouldn't save itself because it wasn't cost effective."
Kurt Vonnegut

I wonder if characters in a novel sense when the end is close, that the last page is just a heartbeat away? Or do they stay wrapped in their minutiae to the very end, counting out their lines, weighing them against each other, blithely unaware of the looming nearness of the back cover?

Some, perhaps, will see the collapse coming and make loose plans for what comes next, but if their Prince Prospero plans, their post-apocalyptic rebuild, does not include Netflix or TikTok, success seems unlikely.

And there will be others who will greet this imminent end with the brainwash of Rapture, wrapping a collective phallus with pages of sacred text and jerking in a repeated upward motion.

But most will be paying only the most desultory attention as long as there is still cash in the ATM, still another episode of *British Bake-Off*, still one more rally where they can confuse enemies losing with victory.

Unlike the dinosaur, we have crafted our own asteroid, called it down upon us, then sit in stunned, uncomprehending wonder as it streaks its way down the sky. We are running out of oil, so we suck harder on the straw. We vote for the fascist screaming about freedom. The world is warming past the point of no return, so we buy an umbrella. Mass shootings so routine they cry out for corporate sponsorship, while in the East, superpowers prepare to play one last, real-life game of Risk.

Collective shrugs of indifference mirror-mock my own wild gestures of frustrated helplessness. I do not know what to do, only what it means. All those academic arguments about the final punctuation, whether period, exclamation point, or question mark, at this close distance, do not matter, and I am left with nothing else but the cold comfort of an unaccountable plot twist:

that after all prophesied dates have come and gone, after all the billions of people—so much more important than I—whose shadows no longer darken the ground, that I will be one of the blessed few granted the firm and final knowledge of how this story ends.

Math Problem

The tragedy of dividing eleven in half
is not that it can't be done evenly;

it is that each half was so
convinced the other was
the one.

The Sadness of Stray Dogs

There is a sadness to stray dogs.
Something that hollows us out,
that whispers of betrayal,
erases our definition of happiness;
the promises of community fall away,
while a charlatan Universe offers
nothing in its stead.

I watch her cross this desolate highway
gridding fallow fields, the occasional farm or
ranch house spotting the landscape
like a coagulated blood-trail of some massive,
long-forgotten beast.
She has no collar, no tag, no leash.
Just swollen dugs, a not-so-subtle reminder that
her plight is legion.

I feel the emptiness of the roller coaster's first drop,
a purging of something I wished to keep. But there is nothing
I can do. My three-room apartment is barely big enough for me.
I cannot fill it with the strays of the world,
no matter how much that idea seduces. There is nothing
I can do, but drive on and hope the sadness does not metastasize,
eat into what I thought was the promise of sunrise.

But the same sunrise scolds me:
She has no collar, no tag, no leash.
She knows nothing of fences or crating.
The futile scribblings of surveyors
mean nothing to her. She walks
and runs and plays to the music of whim,
erasing our definition of happiness;

No collar.
No tag.
And no leash.

Yes, there is a sadness to stray dogs.

But On the Other Hand

If Waldo is so intent on not being
        found,
maybe he should invest in a new
        wardrobe.

Summit

There is a weather here all its own,
made up of rock, dirt, the sweat
of ascent, the angst of avalanche.

Up here, I *feel* at last,
with the understanding of atavism.
There is a coldness on the mountain top
that has nothing to do with wind;
a warmth that has nothing to do with fire,
where one catches a mouthful
of rain from unreliable clouds,
the moisture of which stings with
the memory of rivers.

A surreality of negative space,
magic bracelets that tattoo skin with leached ink,
staining bones long since irrelevant to flesh.
This parallax of time and space,
the air thin as a lost thought,
touched with a whiteness of violet.

Birds of the world vector below me,
with a stale envy of purpose and place,
wondering why I struggled the stone way,
why I misremember the profound gravity
of lightning strike, why the false prophecy
of the smooth shuffle down, to linger
on this patch of barren rock they can visit
on the whim of wing and wind.

In answer, I say to them,
"I do not understand why I am alone up here."
And they reply,
"That is precisely why you are alone up here."

Any Buoyancy Will Do

The problem may be how
we romanticize rescue. We
want it to be the soft strength
of the St. Bernard,
anticipating with calm longing
the warmth of the brandy
from the keg around its neck,

forgetting that any piece
of emotionless plastic that happens
to be nearby and that happens
to float can be a raft,

for it is our own legs,
our own flattened palms,
our own rhythmic panic,
that does most of the work.

Armageddon

1.

The numbers will never be even.
The abundance one-sided.
The Horn of Plenty,
that cornucopia of myth,
is only made of wicker.

2.

Lawn sprinklers ballet-jerk
across a lawn during a spring
Oklahoma rain storm
in a saturation of savage sufficiency.

3.

A son is excited by a new line
of action figures. His father tells him
to choose which one he will not get;
the boy is forbidden, despite the
cardboard proselytizing-package,
to "collect them all." The father believes
this to be a worthy discipline.

Later in the night, the father will excuse himself
from the house to visit the stable of
streetside whores he keeps on retainer.

4.

A newly-landed Haitian enters a
Miami grocery store, cries at the casual
abundance rainbowed before him,
gasps at the irreverent wastage
suggested by expiration dates.

5.

In the corner of that Oklahoma lawn,
double-saturated by spring storm,
a child stands out of reach of the parabola redundancy,
catching raindrops in his mouth,
savoring the deliciousness of a moment,
blithely unaware he is what Hope looks like.

Innately reveling in the satiety of enough,
he will collect them all, or not,
depending on the internal dictation
of his instinctive whim.

He dances with the raindrops,
dances with himself, material
of the same substance.
Both rivulets lusting for an ocean,
watering the needy along the way.

Self-Checkout

I am growing quite fond of the greeter at Walmart.
He carries his salt and pepper pony-tailed self
with the weary peacefulness of the reassembled.
He's about my age, too young to be haunted
by southeastern jungle; too old to be scoured by desert sand,
but he's a veteran of some war nonetheless;
his eyes stuck in the glimmering, his body in perpetual mid-sigh,
it is clear he's been through some deep, unrelenting shit
(shit deeper and more unrelenting than working for Walmart).
And now he spends his days sitting on a stool,
intermittently blasted by Oklahoma wind,

somehow, buffeted from the ritualized indifference
of conglomerate consumers,
somehow, huddled up against some hidden warmth.

I sense he does not do this for the paycheck,
that he takes away something else from conveyor-belt encounters
with depersonalized shoppers who had to become
momentary, unwilling colleagues,
who will post their complaints on social media
about having to check themselves out and then submit
to the implicatory checking of receipts,
who continue, daily and forevermore,
within a fog of their own acceptance.

What value these ceaselessly repeating interactions hold for him I do
not know.
He stands at the liminal, what is left to us of Keats's nightingale,
Shelley's skylark, opaque and inaccessible.
What he can possibly take away from these encounters, I cannot
glean.

But with every curiosity-laden exchange,
every altruistic affirmation (he was quite proud of me
—his words—after learning how Topo Chico
has helped weaned me off soda),
every salutation of "welcome back, brother,"
every time he pauses the machine,

while deep within the belly of the machine
(I mean, this *is* Walmart after all),
after every one of these few-second connections,
these particles of the genuine,
breaths gulped down like I'm a drowning swimmer resurfaced,
these reminders of what the machine is designed to destroy,
I feel I'm just a little bit closer to figuring it out.

Longing for Contact

"the actual world! . . . Contact! Contact!"
Henry David Thoreau

There are people in the world who do not flinch
when a bug lands on them, who are not provoked
into the reactive violence of lethal palm strike
or the more calmly-calculating finger-flick.

There are people who understand
the honeybee's inquisitive visit
is perhaps the highest compliment;
people who serenely submit
to the tender massaging of ant and caterpillar,
who do not fear the spider's fangs
nor the wasp's sting.

I am not one of them.
I still panic at possibility,
still flinch at touch,
still strike before I can even process
which tiny brother or sister has landed,
its message from the world forever unopened.

I am trying to be better, trying
to behave in harmony with the grace
of their unassuming acceptance,
their recognition that I am no different
from the rock, the tree, the soil;
that this is not just as it should be,
but is beautifully so. In their caress
is an offer of transference.
"Do not separate," they skywrite
onto this expanse of skin.

There are people in the world who do not overreact,
do not misinterpret these unexpected invitations,
these opportunities to connect to a world beyond ourselves,
these gentle reminders that so much has so little to do with us.

Yes, there are people in the world like this.
I want to be One.

How a Heart Heals

Annulment: A Love Poem

By some miracle, on par, perhaps, with the one about the loaves and fishes, or the other one involving a virgin birth, my mother attained an annulment after seventeen years of marriage and two teenaged children. To this day, I have no idea how she pulled this off.

"One thing I have to say about your mother," my father once tried to explain, "is she could suck the white off a cue ball. Maybe that's how?" But my brief stint as an altar boy at St. Rita's was enough for me to know such enticements were of no interest to Father Dougan and the rest of the clergy.

She said she did it so she could get married in a church again, a privilege she has yet, forty plus years after the miracle, to take advantage of.

For Father Dougan, it meant I could no longer take Communion, that I would need to find the new religion of no religion.

As for me, it gilded me in nothingness. An annulment makes something null and void; it negates, it invalidates. An annulled marriage is considered never to have existed. Ecclesiastical codification of how I have often felt, of what I've often wished.

In the years that followed, I became a student of nothingness, an aficionado. The suicide attempt an unfortunate but perhaps predictable effort to make this distinction permanent.

There are moments, though, flickered like distant candlelight on a once-sacred wall, when I find myself, by some miracle, on par, perhaps, with the one about the loaves and fishes, or the other one involving a virgin birth, content within the shadowy substance of nothingness, the presence one maintains within an echo, within a shimmer, that delivers more than the banishing world withholds. It is within the clod, scorned by the gold and the silver around it, that the flower, which one day you may place in your hair, shall grow.

Yes, Deer

I sit for a while on an incongruent
bench deep in alpine woods
along the spine of Nevada's Snake Mountains
to catch my breath.

Mt. Wheeler looms behind me,
somehow both maternal and malevolent.
A small brace of mule deer straddle
the trail, float among the birch
like a late morning fog.

While deer usually greet an intrusion
into their woods with indignant surprise,
head jerking up and around
like someone just farted in a room
of polite company,
these look over at me from time to time,
as if checking on whether I am paying
attention. There are lessons to be learned here,
if I am quiet,
if I am observant:

That my shortness of breath is not because the air is too thin.
That I have carried too much weight with me.
That if there is not grass where I stand,
there is certainly some nearby,
often just a few steps away.

And that if I just stop for a while, and rest,
the thing I am chasing will catch up.

The Looming Darkness That Too Often Threatens to Define Us

On the Eve

December 31, 2024

Introspection is difficult
in these final, lingering, remnants
of the year.

The park across the street a launching pad
for illegal fireworks until that ruckus,
predictable and frustrating as it is,
gives way to something more sinister.

Decades of action flicks have trained me
to appreciate the staccato of full automatic fire,
but one does not anticipate that academic knowledge
morphing into manifestation on one's street corner.
A clip is emptied, a new clip inserted,
and the sky fire continues over and again.

The insensate terror of Parkland and Uvalde,
the haunting echo within the school halls
of Sandy Hook and Columbine,
co-opted into drunken celebration of an arbitrary calendar turn.

The gunfire is joined from an opposite corner of the park,
the rapid pop of pistol emptied and then—
because the dance is the same everywhere—
another clip inserted and emptied.
Spaced booms from a revolver elsewhere help keep the beat,
pacing this most American symphony.

There is no way to tell if this is celebration still
or now something more malevolent.
Our malice, our casual cruelty,
has become so metastatic that it is difficult
to tell the difference.

Yesterday I read in the news of a man in critical condition
after being pushed by a stranger onto subway tracks.
Earlier this holiday month, a homeless woman was set on fire

as she slept in a subway car.
In New Orleans tonight, someone drove a car into revelers,
killing fourteen of them.
And in a parkside Oklahoma City neighborhood,
gunfire splits this last night and no one
(myself included) calls the police.

The sounds of violence simply an unquestioned fact of life tonight,
as if, for these few moments, I am Ukrainian,
as if, for these few moments, I am Palestinian.

Is it coming for us now?
Is it already here?
What we can tolerate knows no bounds.
Both our blessing and our curse.

Introspection is difficult
in these final, lingering, remnants
of the year.
But in the beats of silence
while street-corner celebrants reload,
what else is left us to do?

A Good Death

The Norsemen had it right:
It is to be found only on the battlefield.

I take issue, however,
with their too-narrow understanding
of what a battlefield looks like.

In Which Paul Discovers That Not All Platitudes Are Platitudinous

Sipping first morning coffee,
watching the stars sheath themselves
into nascent light.

A robin descends
onto the small strip
of grass before my landing,
a worm dangling from its beak.

"I'll be damned," I whisper
into the silence of yet another
instructive morning.

Put Me In, Coach

There is a cemetery in Utah called Centerfield.
How nice, if that is what Death is like.
An expanse of well-manicured grass,
as far away from the foul lines as it's possible to get.
No fear of errors or missed cut-off men;
no worry about runners tagging up,
for the ball you caught was the final out.

Based on the cemetery's size,
I don't think admission is proscriptively literal.
Not only are fellow outfielders invited,
but so, I assume, is the armored catcher
and his lanky battery mate.
The nimble middle infielder and the utility men,
blanketing the absence of depth with their resplendent versatility,
brazen third basemen, well-intentioned coaches,
managers gilded in omniscience,
are all invited to gambol here, under this field of final rest.
Perhaps even thick, rectangular first basemen like me,
forever stretching for a ball that never seems to get there,
will be welcomed.
How nice, if that is what Death is like.

Of course, this changes, rather radically, the John Fogerty song,
makes it significantly more macabre.
The enthusiasm of the singer either disturbingly suicidal
or morbid Rapture-esque fanaticism.
But even so…

In the next town down the road,
the cemetery is called Black Rock Eternal Rest,
a name much more in keeping with
with my expectations:
the blackness of a void,
the weight of stone,
and an unchanging eternity.

I want to turn around,
to make *this* choice, at least,

thinking all the while:
How nice.
If that is what Death is like.

Metaphysics

Perhaps the greatest argument
against the sham belief in Free Will
is that no matter my rigid determination
not to do so, when I listen
to Steve Miller's "Take the Money and Run,"
I do the clappy thing.

Both times.

Thoughts of a Useful Idiot: A Prose Persona Poem

The other day, I was called a "useful idiot" by Benjamin Netanyahu. He stood behind a podium in the Capital building of *my* country and lectured *me* about my right to protest his genocide. For a few days, I struggled to get past the sheer *balls* on this guy. He tells me I'm siding "with murderers and rapists" while every day murder is committed under his direction and in his name.

Imagine for a moment Hitler or Stalin—and if you feel I'm being too dramatic with those choices, I would suggest the difference is merely one of degree, not kind—but still, if you prefer, let's say Pol Pot, Mladic, Bagosora, Talaat Pasha, et cetera (and if you had to look up any of those names, you are making several points for me); imagine one of them standing behind the podium in the House chamber, scolding us for an "over-reaction."

I've had a few days to settle down now. And I've come to the realization that Netanyahu is half right. The part he got wrong was the "useful" bit.

I have not proven very useful in preventing missile strikes against schools and hospitals, nor have I been very useful in preventing the digging of mass graves, into which Palestinian women and children are hidden, fallow seeds in a macabre garden that will harvest rancorous fruit. Nor was I able to assist NICU nurses maneuvering dozens and dozens of isollettes through the unhermetic, rubble-strewn streets of Gaza, and I have proven downright useless at preventing the death of hundreds of international aid workers killed by Israeli munitions, or the continual execution of Palestinian doctors, or the horrific game of Whack-A-Mole Netanyahu revels in playing with his "safe zones" and refugee camps. And my inefficiency at explaining to supporters of the war effort that Palestinians are not *starving*, they are *being starved*, knows no bounds. About the only thing I've proved useful at is boycotting McDonald's; in other words, useful at a useless thing.

That said, I am indeed an idiot. Netanyahu got that part right.

I am an idiot for hearing the post-Holocaust phrase, "Never Again," and thinking it represented an unshakable resolve. A line in the sand we, collectively, would never let be crossed. Even after Cambodia. Even after Rwanda. Even after Darfur. Even after every subsequent cleansing. Even as the whispers built into crescendo then clarion then coda, screaming the unassailable truth that when we said, "Never Again," we only meant white people.

And I am an idiot for not understanding (although it is truly not understanding I lack, but acceptance) that the intentionally-disingenuous moral relativism that uses the Hamas attacks to gild *everything* that follows with a paper tiger-thin veneer of justification, is an argument Americans have been long conditioned to embrace (see: Wounded Knee, Dresden, Tokyo, Nagasaki, et cetera).

And I am an idiot to think the brokers of war could see the blowback inevitabilities of bombs labelled "made in the U.S.A." dropped on Gazan schools and soccer fields, that the wanton destruction of a people offers *nothing* in the way of peace, only adds fuel to an unquenchable fire.

And I am an idiot for thinking that, goddamn it, it is high time we found a way to quench that fire.

So, yes, Bibi, maybe you're right. Maybe I am useful idiot. But at the end of the day, I think I would rather be a useful idiot than a useless son of a bitch, which is how *you* will be remembered in history books, sitting on your blood-stained hands in a group photo of infamy. Look to your left, Bibi. That's Omar al-Bashir. On your right, Andrew Jackson. See their smiles, their welcoming eyes. They are happy to welcome you to the club. They feel proud to be sitting next to you. How will *you* feel sitting next to them?

On TV

"I reported what I saw and heard, but only part of it.
For most of it, I have no words."
Edward R. Murrow

The dodo went extinct sometime during
the mid- to late-sixteen hundreds.
There's no certainty about the exact day,
the exact time. The last recorded sighting
was in 1662, but the passing of the species
went unnoticed, unheeded,
in the island isolation of Mauritius.

We have a bit more clarity about
the passenger pigeon. Once so numerous
a flock in flight would blot out the sun,
the last one died on the first of September, 1914,
in a cage in the Cincinnati Zoo.
They even gave the last one a name: Martha,
although having an identity
did not pause or prevent its passing.

So many extinctions happen off-camera,
the exact node separating the time
when something existed
and when it ceases to be,
unmarked and unwitnessed.

It is the same with genocide.
In fact, genocide depends on this,
depends on living in the shadow of rumor
that seems far too often hyperbole,
banks on our collective atrocity fatigue,
our suspicion of round numbers.

That is why journalists were expelled
from Rwanda in the mid-90s;
why technology was an anathema
in Cambodia, why it took
Edward R. Murrow's words
to crystalize for us Buchenwald.

We have no such limitations,
nor the excuses they offer,
in Gaza today. Nor do we need
to rely on a reporter's words.
The lack thereof Murrow descries
can be no barrier to an understanding
of the systematic horrors
of which we are capable.

For we have images.
We see them on our TVs screens
each evening, often pixelated because,
as the news anchors warn,
"some of the images may be disturbing."
And perhaps that is the problem:
we need to be disturbed more.

When the hospitals were first bombed,
when the mandated evacuation routes were first bombed,
when the refugee camps were first bombed,
when the schools were first bombed,
when the children
        and the women
        and the elderly
        and the infirm were
        first bombed
(all with names,
although having an identity
did not pause or prevent their passing),
I assumed this could not go on for long.
Surely this time would be different.
Because this extinction,
this cleansing,
this genocide
is being played out on TV.

But I failed to account
for the ease with which
we can change the channel.
Forgot that *Real Housewives of Orange County* starts at 7:00,
that *Survivor* comes on at 8:00.

On Grieving

One summer in my youth,
two boys snuck into the Bronx Zoo
at night. They were found
the next morning, dead, partially consumed,
in the polar bear enclosure.

On the news, they speculated
it was the heat, the unrelenting
humidity of the city drove the boys
to swim in cold water.

The one bear caught
in the halo of crepuscular light
standing over the bodies, was
immediately put down.

On the news, they speculated
this was done to minimize risk
to keepers from a predator with a taste
now for the sweetness of our flesh.

The second bear they left alone.
It spent the rest of the summer walking
in an invisible track, six steps forward,
six steps in reverse. It did not eat, rarely slept,
ignored the essentiality of cold water.

It just walked in an invisible track.
Six steps forward, six steps in reverse.
Over and again, until it gave up and died.
Zoo officials labeled this death "natural causes."

On the news, no speculation was offered.
The story was long over, the focus moved on.
I have no doubt the "natural causes" part
is true, although perhaps not quite
the way the zoo officials meant it.

What quality of life is left after
the thing that made it bearable
is taken? How does one break free
from sorrow and loss?

Questions posed decades of summers ago
I am just now trying to answer.
An adumbrate lesson Nature offers
with the impossible hope we don't
have to learn such things first-hand.

New Love

I watch them shuffle across the park, in no discernable hurry, unconcerned with destination, a stark contrast to their brindled hound, who spends the time bounding after shadowy whisp of squirrel and previous dog, the mythology of scent amalgamated into legend, running with its ears and tail up, alert. Still young.

They are not. She, crooked like a straw; he, frayed like a long-forgotten blanket. They shuffle across the park. Together. In no discernable hurry. He, always a few paces ahead, sherpa-like. I would prefer they walked alongside each other, yet note with muted joy that regardless, they walk together every day. The how is less important. And my preference less important still.

I don't know their story, so I invent one: They've been married twenty years. This is the second marriage for each. They chose poorly the first time. They chose to wait for the moment, but then the moment passed them by. So they waited for it to return. And now they shuffle, together, across the park. In no discernable hurry, unconcerned with destination.

They are regular visitors. They usually park on the other street, across the green field and the still-river asphalt of walkpath. But today, they park outside my window, so I am able to see the look, the one she gives him once the dog is loaded back in the car. A look of gratitude and promise and longing and calm completeness. And, for the unobserved observer in the window, pedagogy:

Love need not grow old, though we do. It pushes against staleness, renewed daily at the fount. By a daily shared walk or a poem or a quiet moment sitting on steps, looking for Orion. New love is not a function of time. It is fed by a different stream: the return of seasons, the continual remergence of the Sun, the steady presence of the moon. It is in no discernable hurry, unconcerned with destination.

Fame

Finding one of your own books
on a dusty shelf of a used bookstore
means two things:

You have officially reached a certain
low rung level of fame;
and there is at least one
person who is not at all impressed.

A Last Hurrah

After years ensconced in a communal association with ice and galvanized rubber, I tried to return again to the world of grass and leather, asked a celebrated coach of the local Legion team, a team laden with friends and former teammates, for a tryout. He gave me five pitches. "I don't see you playing a fucking inning," he concluded.

But he was looking at the wrong things. He saw five pitches.

And if he'd been able look into the future and see the stolen bases, how every walk, every admittedly rare single cocooned into a triple; or if he was able to see how the hockey goalie had mastered the stretch, that alchemist's trick turning hits into outs, he would *still* be looking at the wrong things.

He saw five pitches. He did not see the eighteen-year-olds around him as eighteen-year-olds, with one last summer to be such. He did not see that many of us would never play again, and the few who would, would never play together. Or if he did see, he forgot what it meant.

He was right about one thing, though. I did not play a fucking inning.

I played twenty.

Halls of Fame: Thoughts on the Death of Pete Rose

So many people clamoring for Pete
to get into Cooperstown,
and I say why not put him in?
We have so many rapists already in our Halls of Fame,
their plaques and busts exalted beside murderers and abusers,
that really, what's one more?

We immortalize what we value.
And surely, it is more important
that someone runs fast,
has a cannon for an arm,
can defy gravity while dunking.

More important, all of this,
than decency (for which there is no Hall of Fame,
I will note merely *sotto voce*,
for I do not wish to offend
those grieving Pete's passing,
those for whom these words seem too soon).

As we do with all the others,
Kobe, Roethlisberger, O.J. and all the rest,
we will, Pontious-like, wash our hands
with declarations like:
"this place is not about him as a person
but as a player,"
as if the player is not still the person;

we will think to ourselves:
"Sure, I would have *preferred*
Rose not fuck thirteen-year-old girls,
but man, could he hit a fast ball."

We know we cannot say this out loud,
so we find other ways to say this out loud,
like building Halls of Fame;
like putting Rose and his brethren in them.

And, of course, think of all the victims,
the legions of the sexually assaulted,
the beaten and the abused,
think of the comfort they will surely feel after each enshrinement,
how proud they will be to have been so close
to a piece of history, to some unquestioned
achievement of glory.

How lucky they will surely feel,
then.

Totality

April 8, 2024

So often, final moments pass into blinked afterimage unnoted.
Our last trip to an amusement park, a beach, or the post office,
the last time we experience the physicality of love-touch,
the last time we savor our favorite dish, with a glass of heady wine,
or sit on a favorite bench;
our last smile with a good friend,
our last joke-laugh or poetry reading,
all of these move along adorned in supplicant robes,
hope routined into casual assumption,
while sand in an ageless timer counts down,
and the Fates silently sharpen their scissors in vigil.

But not today.
Today is different.
I know enough celestial mechanics to understand.
Staring at the haloed black orb above,
I know exactly what it is I see.

Restitution

When the day of reckoning comes,
I hope a few friends will put
in a good word for me.
But if they are too occupied to do so,
I will try to understand.

Murrah

The marathon route goes right by my apartment,
adding an unusual cheering section to my morning ritual
of coffee and poetry on an otherwise solitary landing.

A carnival of plastic horns and New Years' noisemakers
challenge my reading. Spectators carry picnic baskets and signs,
fathers give sons piggyback rides,
echoes of phantom pressure on now solitary shoulders.
Someone has turned their lawn sprinklers outward,
bathing the runners in cooling mist.
Some of them are just walking at this point,
fatigued far from the finish.

It's hard not to think of Murrah and McVeigh today.
Perhaps because he kept the name of a child until the end,
or maybe because I have too much darkness in my life already,
I try to think of him as a small boy,
lacking the applause that should accompany childhood.
Those communal celebrations of Little League and birthday parties,
where it did not matter if you got a hit,
or what you wished for,
because it is never the result we applaud,
because so much can be achieved by the placing together of hands.

I put down my book and go inside for a better view of the
celebration.
I want to write about this pushback against the darkness,
this reclaiming of a nightmare, but divorce relocated me here
only four years ago. To me,
the bombing was a tragic news story, played out on a TV screen.
I feel this is not my story to tell, not my poem to write.
I worry there are griefs that should not be appropriated.

I'll watch from the window for a while longer, I decide,
then return to my cramped landing and to my reading,
grateful for the company, and for the applause,
even if it is not for me.

Blithe Air

"my head bathed in the blithe air,
and uplifted into infinite space,
all mean egotism vanishes"
Ralph Waldo Emerson

There is a party across the way,
about three dozen people
of varying ages gathered
under the park's pavilion and
across the open, grassed plain—
green-soaked from early-November
drought-busting deluge—surrounding.

The music is respectfully-volumed,
loud enough for me to know it exists,
but too distant to catalog its form or its content.

They have brought food and bundles
of red and white balloons,
are as casually unconcerned by the one red balloon
that got away, the less-dense air inside
drifting it higher and higher above this
secular congregation until the pressure
of the world above their little patch of joy
will cause it to explode,
as I am (for it is not my balloon, after all).

A *quinceañera*, perhaps, or a child's birthday,
I cannot quite tell from this middle distance.
Something, certainly, that celebrates
the joy of youth, its stubborn insistence
on denying substance or weight to
the looming darkness that too often
threatens to define us.

I am not one of them, nor need I be.
There can be only so much
that is provincial in a public park.
(And did I not watch with them their
wayward balloon, surprisingly untinged

by the usual sadness of childhood memory?)
Like a pond rippling after a pebble
lands in its midst, part of the party's purpose,
whatever that purpose is, reaches me.
For while I am not invited to share in the joy
of this particular celebration, it is enough
(for now, at least) to know
that there are celebrations still.

The Poem Gina Sweetly, Kindly, and Graciously Reminded Me to Write Because I Promised on Facebook to Write a Poem about Barbie and I am Clever, Witty and Sublime Enough to Write a Poem About Barbie (Gina's Suggested Title);

Or

For All the CEO's Who Spent Tuesday, April 9, 2024 Bitching About the Lost Revenue Impact of Employees Taking the Day Off to Watch the Solar Eclipse.

It's all about the packaging, how Barbie is marketed in bright pink boxes, with mandated occupational labels like "Pop Star Barbie" and "Nurse Barbie." There is no "Gaslit Barbie" nor "Battered Girlfriend Barbie" (I checked Amazon) because play is supposed to be pretend;

boxes adorned with demands gilded as encouragement—"collect them all"—because play must feed the machine, must reaffirm hidden corporate manifestos. Else, what is the point?

The strictures of play so proscriptive one must push through guilt in order to enjoy, and even then, some sticks like a determined burr, calling into question the value of play itself, because the machine will only wait so long.

If one is not careful, titles of poems can work this way too. Commissioned ones, especially. Hidden among the lack of consistent Oxford commas is a fence, limiting what can be written about and what cannot. This morning, lingering within sleep-drowse despite repeated coffee-fuel dosing, the pressures of Gina's request are palpable.

I could ponder the implications of Gerwig's and Robbie's Oscar snubs, question whether they would even *want* an award that looks like a golden phallus.

I could wander within self-reflective hopes that I am more Alan than Ken.

I could be clever, witty, and/or sublime (Gina would most certainly opt, probably with great justice, for the word "dishonest") and write about a different Barbie, my work colleague, perhaps, who often delightfully distracts with conversation, or that waitress at a diner just outside Memphis who lingers in my mind for reasons I cannot fully account for but may have something to do with that meal being one of the last I shared with my son, a mid-week road trip when I should have been working.

I think what I will do, though, is throw my hands up and declare to Gina that I was unable to write the poem she asked for, maybe ask for some limited forgiveness.

But I will most certainly thank her for the challenge, resulting as it did in time spent this morning at play instead of grading papers;

play, which always comes bundled within its own justification,
play that is never defined by an end product,
play that cannot be proscribed or mandated away.

The machine, the voice of the whimsical child hidden within reminds us at any opportunity, can wait
for the poem,
for the road trip,
for the eclipse
to have its day
and to have its say.

Else, what is the point?

Understanding John Venn in Ely, Nevada

There's not much to do in Ely, Nevada except find yourself. The valleys are wide and sparse. The mountain ranges walling them in, looming and vast. Cutting through the valley, the mountains, the town, is The Loneliest Road in America. On any given day, you'll see more elk and mule deer than people.

This, of course, is exactly why I'm here.

Like a groundhog in February, I prefer to see only my own shadow. But I still have to eat occasionally, so I leave the hotel room, my Fortress of Solitude (although I am no Superman) this past week of alpine hiking, and walk to the Mexican restaurant across the street.

I want only the most cursory conversation:
> What do I want to drink, to eat?
> Will there be anything else?
> Pay at the register.
> Thank you.

But my server is on me like a Jack Russell scenting a fox. Hails me as a fellow longhair. I make a joke about my bald spot, prophesy he'll dodge this unfortunate genetic bullet. He asks about my T-shirt, and so we discuss Thoreau. Before I leave, he points to the bangles and bracelets adorning my wrists, the ones I wear to keep the urge to singe skin with cigarettes waveringly at bay, and asks if we can do an exchange, pulling off his string of turquoise beads in anticipation of my answer.

Despite the heavy meal of carne asada and beans, the walk back is lightsome, haloed by this unexpected—for in Ely, Nevada there's not much to do but find yourself—reminder that this is a Venn world, a further reminder of the need to keep a foot in both circles. This unexpected gift, this reversed gratuity, far better than any souvenir or memento offered in any of the stores I've driven by on this long, long trip down The Loneliest Road in America.

Who Wants an RV Anyway?

The marquee read:
"We Let You Name Your Own Down Payment."

I said I'd like to name mine Fernando.

They asked me to leave.

Line Drive in the Box Score

While cleaning out my garage,
removing the detritus of a life
one cold December morning,
I find it leaning in a cobwebbed corner:
My old, belovedly-battered,
highlighter-orange softball bat.

They say it takes one thousand hits
to fully-break in a new one (a truth
not limited, I suppose, to just bats).
It's frayed-tape handle, the innumerable
scuff marks scouring and scarring its
barrel tell a story blanketed now in the
faded haze of retreating memory.

What was its final hit?
I can no longer remember.
Did it launch that yellow ball
over the fence 270 feet away
(for there were a few of those)?
Or was it a more linear drive into the gap?
Perhaps a smoked grounder past a suddenly timid
third-baseman, or a parabola blooped
down the first base line
when the other team over-shifted,
labelling me (with some justice)
an unrepentant pull hitter?

Too much time has passed.
The games of boys played by men who refuse
to grow old are no longer proffered.
I can no longer remember.
And those who came to watch me play
are no longer around to remind me.

I'm surprised to find the stick
still feels good, feels right, in my hands,
beguiling me with the thought
I could pick up where I left off.

But the cobwebs, the near-empty garage,
the apartment just as empty above it,
whisper another story.

They say it takes one thousand hits
to fully-break in a new one (a truth
not limited, I suppose, to just bats).
Cleaning out my garage,
removing the detritus of a life
one cold December morning,
I can no longer remember my last hit,
not knowing it would be my last.

I Took Down the Pictures of My Sons Today

I took down the pictures
of my sons today,
flat rectangles of
what they looked like
five years ago, after-image
from an ex-life,
partisan-chronicled.

Like a spaceman past
the point of no return,
or a crash survivor tossed
violently into the rain forest
when he expected to
land safely in Sacramento,
I have been given this
world to survive in. It
does no good to long for
the one lost behind.

Hole-Hearted

Walking a deserted trail near
a still and silent lake on a
cold mid-February morning,
I came across a tree with a hole
in its center. A near-perfect circle,
far too large for beetle violence;
far too symmetrical for the rage
of some long-forgotten Oklahoma storm.

A wound caused by arbitrary distance,
maybe, or a strain of narcissism,
or possibly something more petty,
a preference for Pepsi perhaps.
But whatever caused the sunder,
the cost was this tree's heart.

How wondrous that despite
the lingering stamp of absence,
this tree continues to grow,
gave up on the idea of filling the hole
and just grew around it. Despite
such determination, surely there is
still pain coursing through the tree,
making its growth inconsistent and hard.

How much more so, then,
for those of us
not made of wood?

I Heard a Woodpecker in Oklahoma City

I heard a woodpecker in the heart of Oklahoma City this morning.

I did not see it, but seeing a woodpecker is never the point. I sat, like
I try to do most days, on my landing, cup of coffee cooling too fast
for my preference on this early-Spring morning, listening:

I heard the hydraulic hiss of the public bus, disgorging riders,
consuming more.
I heard a dog, lodging complaints in rhythmic protest, a cadence
occasionally taken up by
       comrades across the neighborhood.
I heard a constant vehicular susurrus, interrupted, on a few
occasions, by the more panicked
       insistence of siren and air horn
       or the over-revved compensation of muscle car motors.
I heard the neighbors two homes down, their dissonance of morning
argument.
I heard the Doplered roar of Southwest jets and the thrumming
whine of landscaper tools.
From the park across the street, I heard the staccato of dribbling and
the vibrating clang of ball
       meeting rim.
I heard the routine, unavoidable tremolo and vibrato of the city, a
sycophantic symphony, what
       my poet friend once termed overwhelming evidence of a
"noisome humanity."

But also, on this early-Spring morning, with a cup of coffee that,
while cooling too fast for my preference, was still warm, I heard a
woodpecker in the heart of Oklahoma City.

Only Just Now Learning to Breathe

Anagnorisis

Poets often have a difficult time with WebMD.
Our fixation with word choice often makes
diagnosis difficult; our wonder and our concern
often detoured by language.

We would describe the sensation behind our eyelids
      as "fluttering,"
label the pulsing in what we paranoically fear
must be our cancer-ridden colon
      as a "flexing."
Our tendons and joints sing to us
in a song we find heroic,
      not predictive;
while the difference between "sore" and "pain"
becomes a metaphor for a future poem
      rather than a practical gauge.

Trained for so long to search for the precise, right word,
and if we can' t find a word that fits,
to make up a new one that does,
it is hard to remember that WebMD,
and perhaps the world at large,
does not use language this way.

We want to know what is wrong with us,
so that we can use word and image to corral it,
reframe it in a way that provides perspective for us
and maybe even comfort for others.

It is easy to interpret the lack of search results
as proof there is no disease or injury
that the fluttering and the flexing
are just figments of our professional,
over-stimulated, imaginations.
Which, of course, they are.
Even, perhaps especially, when they are not.

Postcards

Invocation: Once More Unto the Breach

My mistake was thinking one trip
would do it.
That last year's sojourn through
New Mexico, Arizona, and
Colorado would be enough to soothe
a troubled soul.

So many things that fell into place
last year have been
jostled loose once again.

And like a vaccine that needs
a booster, I'm on the move again,
driving new roads, revisiting
old favorites.

Once again, I head west.

(Because she lives in the west,
and one of these trips I will
reach her.
But not yet.
That is not the point of this trip.)

I see in the faces of some of my friends
worry at my leave-taking.
An uncertainty. They sense that one day
I may leave on one of these trips and
not return.
I do not think it will be this trip.
It is not Grey Havens time.
Not yet.

And so I have come back to you,
western roads, in hopes
you will finish what you started.

Day 1: Through Western Oklahoma to Cañon City, CO, with an afternoon stop at Capulin Volcano National Monument

Postcard One: Object Lesson

Like a dry sponge first time dampened, I soak up West Oklahoma.
Ocean grain rolling to panhandle wind. The uninspired naming of Ft.
Supply. A blue heron in unhurried flight skimming above its creek
bed reflection. Road signs of existential uncertainty, like "Road May
Flood." A red tractor silhouetted on a ridge outside Seiling.

I stop at an All-Sups to buy a Red Bull as a hedge against future
weariness. The woman behind the counter asks if I'm a storm chaser.
She explains "because you're dressed so flamboyant." This is the first
time in my life I've been called "flamboyant." She sees the necklaces,
the bracelets, the Hawaiian shirt given to me by a friend and thinks I
chase storms. And I do. Just not the ones she means.

There's a group of beautiful women in the parking lot. Because I've
been reading a lot of Bukowski lately, I ponder how nice it would be
to join them in one of his poems. Instead, I try to disregard their
mermaid songs, fill up my tank, and drive on. A few miles later, I'm
climbing a stegosaurus in Woodward. Someone yells that the park is
for kids. As if I did not know that already.

Postcard Two: Crater's Edge

In the afternoon New Mexico sun, I perch on a volcano's rim,
rubbing what was once stardust between my fingers. A short while
before, I took the strenuous hike along the crater's rim, the heart-
pounding and the piñon, the shortness of breath and the juniper
reminding me I'm still alive. I get small, odd looks from the families
and the couples along the trail, in the parking lot. They are wondering
what story this solitary greying man has to tell. It is an old story. And
there is no need to tell it. Instead, I sit on the crater's edge, listen to

its secrets. Wind-weathered and worn, it whispers that while change can be cataclysmic, but it need not always be.

Day 2: Pikes Peak

Postcard Three: Not Yet

I wake up sore from yesterday's hike. A good sore, welcomed like an old friend, a reminder that some things are not yet out of reach. The morning finds me less than an hour from Pikes Peak. Three years ago, I tried to get to the summit and failed. Inspiration, the invigoration of aching muscle, the hint of accomplishment they whisper, determines me for another essay.

Racing the sun to the top, I push past mile 16, where my son and I turned back three years ago, discover the road beyond is less scary, and soon reach the summit. At the bottom of the road, a park ranger told me, "When you get up there, remember to breathe," and now, this close to the sky, I understand the advice. Reaching out, plucking a cloud from the thin blue around me seems as simple as adjusting a shirt collar, or pony-tailing hair against unrelenting wind.

Three years ago, I tried to get to the summit and failed. Now, I stand rubber-legged and dizzy in lightsome air. The morning's lesson returns: Some things are not yet out of reach. My son is not with me this time, nor the "unknown her" of the poem I wrote after that failed attempt. I note their absence, but am not as bothered by it as I expected.

Three years ago, I tried to get to the summit and failed. It amazes me in that time how little healing has occurred. And also, how much healing has occurred.

Day 3: Rangely, CO to Nephi, UT

Postcard Four: The Comfort of Routine

It takes 4.5 hours to get to Nephi from here.
I plan to take all day.
But not yet.

First, I invite my old friend Habit to join me on my cabin's porch (a stand-in for my apartment's landing). It's early, and the other guests are not out or about yet, so, as it is most mornings, it's just me, a steaming mug of coffee, and a collection of poems. Between Bukowski, I watch a new but familiar sunrise, look at a different set of trees I can't identify. The morning quiet broken only by the barking of a distant dog, a cheeky raven who seems personally offended by my reading choice, and a kid on an ATV cutting across the lodge's back lot. I'm reflexively bothered by this last intrusion, but he's entitled, I suppose, to connect to this morning in his own way. He heads off into the erasure of mesa and the engine whine wanes back into morning quiet again.

Just the raven occasionally voicing its displeasure, and the turning of pages.

Postcard Five: Breakfast for Two

Before my goodbye to Colorado, I pull off onto a gravel shoulder to have breakfast in the north desert mesa. Sitting in the open hatch with a gas station burrito, among the caves and crevasses, plinths and rippled rock, formations that look like they were zippered together long ago, then stretched out and abandoned, I hear the ear-ringing silence of eons working at their own pace. Until a raven lands nearby. Perhaps it is the same one from the porch; perhaps a different one, hoping I'll drop some food. After a few moments of mutual contemplation, it caws. I don't speak raven, but it sounds like a question.

"You're right," I answer, dropping the last of the tortilla on the ground as an offering, and get back on the road.

Postcard Six: Lost

I miss my turn outside Duchesne and have to double back. Before I right my course, I stop at a pull-off, read the historic marker, spend a few moments on a bridge, gazing at the impossibly blue of Strawberry Reservoir. In this land of soil stratified, red and tan and white and yellow and gray, the striking contrast of the bright cerulean momentarily blinds.

According to the marker, on September 19, 1776, two Spanish priests trying to find a new route linking Santa Fe to Monterey, doubted their native guides. They thought they were lost. They were wrong. As is usually the case.

Postcard Seven: Anointed

I didn't think there could be a path to rival the stark splendor of Rt 191, where I pulled off for a simple lunch of bread and tomato within towering ridges of wind-hewn sandstone. But then whimsy steers me to Rt 31, winding up and through Monti-La Sal National Forest. The sky along this alpine pass seems so perfectly fake it must be a bluescreen. Hillsides of purple and yellow wildflowers in the shadow of young white birch. I pass the body of a roadkill fox, and even it was beautiful. Alongside the trilling of a small creek in North Hughes Canyon, I rinse my feet, recall the advice the ranger at Pikes Peak gave me yesterday, and remind myself to breathe.

Day 4: Nephi, UT to Ely, NV

Postcard Eight: Endorheic

There is a lake in southwest Utah that is not really a lake. Sevier Lake is charitably called an "intermittent" lake, despite the fact that it has been mostly dry during its recorded history. The stretch of US Highway 50, running from Delta, Utah to Fernley, Nevada, which runs past the lake, is called "The Loneliest Road in America." Blanketing a small corner of this vibrantly monochromous high desert, the lake does not look like water, seems more some kind of viscous erasure, a giant roll of Visqueen pulled taut against mountainside. Along its edges, patches of white gypsum look like snowbank. Additional research gave me the term "endorheic," which means the lake does not drain into other bodies of water. It just sits there, in the scalding Sevier Desert, waiting on the erasure of evaporation. Since 2011, it has never exceeded a depth of three feet. On the atlas I carry, it is not even colored blue. Just outlined. Its salinity is two and half times that of ocean water, and as a result, it never freezes. Some sources peevishly complain that it is nothing more than a source of "wind-blown dust." Those sources are thinking of it in the wrong terms. It is not a body of water. It is a metaphor.

Day 5-7: Great Basin National Park

Postcard Nine: Bristlecone/Alpine Lakes Trail

There is no cell service out here. While there is a profound
satisfaction to be away from the dopamine rush of Facebook likes
and text messages (and the one text I hope for never comes anyway),
there is also a nervousness to these days. Self-awareness demands I
acknowledge that. The unavoidable reality is that I'm 52, will be
hiking by myself, at high-altitude and I'm no longer in hiking shape
(although round *is* a shape, I suppose). And I'll be hiking in remote
areas where things will hunt you. A point the sign in the Visitor's
Center about mountain lions makes clear. One piece of advice the
sign offers is to "avoid hiking alone."

If I had listened to that advice, I wouldn't have walked through a
wildflowered meadow at 11,000 feet. Nor pondered the significance
of ripples on crystal-blue Sarah Lake. I would have missed watching
the wind dance along Sarah's sister, turquoised Teresa, a mile down
the trail. I would not have had to wait forty satisfying minutes for a
brace of mule deer to leave the trail ahead, one doe repeatedly
looking my way, locking eyes, as if checking on my breathing. I
would have missed meeting a 3300-year-old bristlecone pine, born a
thousand years before Christ, would not have felt its lesson of hardy,
graceful patience. I would have missed seeing ice in July, a glacier this
far south proof that anything is possible (including longed-for text
messages).

Yes, I would have missed all of these things, all because of a fear that
barely added to my pack-weight.

Postcard Ten: Lehman Caves

There is a comfort in the subterranean. A lure that brings me back to
the caverns in Carlsbad with a needful regularity. But I am skeptical
of this visit to these more modest caves, guard against that reflexive
cultural need we have to rank. Here, a guided tour is the only option.
I join nineteen other visitors and follow Ranger Grant into the
dimness of a limestone calcite embrace. The tour visits five named
"rooms." In one labelled the Gothic Palace, Ranger Grant turns off
all the NPS lighting, wanting to share with us total darkness. An
atavistic unease spreads among the group. Trepidation quivers just

below fear. But instead, I find comfort here. Something not quite nameable, but recognized. This is not the darkness of despair, but a darkness of complete and total erasure. A reduction of the self to its inviolate essence. I am nothing but a mind and a consciousness. The worries and shames of the body disappear. I am unfettered and real. A good memory to keep with me; a recollection of full self to call upon when needed.

Postcard Eleven: Wheeler Saddle (elevation 11,800 ft)

There are two kinds of people: beach people and mountain people. It's clear which I am. There is something soothingly primal about mountains. The air is just simpler here. If First Principles still exist, are still available to us, this is where they'll be found.

And then there is the symbolism of moving upward, gaining perspective alongside elevation. Negotiating a mountain involves an unlocking, an emptying. And a calibration, preparation for the eventual descent.

Thoreau had his Katahdin, and I understand why his speech failed him there. But it is unfortunate that we associate his transcendent erasure with the summit. The summit is just one aspect of experience. As I rest in Wheeler Saddle, mountain weather greeting my arrival with a light, cooling rain, rinsing sweat and hike-grime from my body like a ritual in an ancient ceremony, I consider the two summits astride me. To the east, Wheeler Peak, rocky and wind-harassed, frowns down at me, as if saying, "What are you waiting for?" There's another mile and a half of trail, another 1,200 feet of elevation. To the west, a much shorter, easier walk to the top of Bald Mountain. I choose neither. The saddle is high enough. The summit is not essential; the mountain is.

Day 8: Ely, NV to Page, AZ

Postcard Twelve: Pendulum

It is raining in the valley. Storm clouds blanket the Steptoe, sagging with rain-weight. To the west, where the storm has finished its work, the Egan Range is snow-capped in cloud; to the east, cotton clouds crest over the Snake Range like volcanic ash. I sense in these signs the directrix. It is time to swing back.

Last year, I turned back in Arizona; this time I nudged into Nevada. In a year, maybe two, I might make it all the way west, embrace, at last, the redwood and whomever is standing beside the redwood. But not yet.

It is important to take a different route back, the journey a circle, not a recrossed line. So I turn off The Loneliest Road in America, head southwest, exchanging mountain for desert, seeking cauterization. The storm had its way with my open sunroof and windows overnight, filling the cabin with humidity, turning me into a storm cloud, descending into arid land.

Day 9: Page, AZ to Gallup, NM

Postcard Thirteen: Cavalier

Ripping into the late morning silence, a kid on a crotch rocket—tired, perhaps, of waiting for a passing lane—whines past a string of cars descending US 89, streaking down the highway on the wrong side of the road, as if daring oncoming traffic to materialize. He weaves back into the right lane recklessly, barely misses clipping my front end. He is soon horizoned, pulling away from the rest of us as if we were parked.

I am struck by his selfishness, the braggart rudeness of this solipsism. The attempt to involve the rest of us in his death is an arrogance that offends. There are any number of mountain tops and mesas around that he could choose. Death is a private place, a cloistered moment, solemn and solitary. Not this showboating loudness, this braggadocio.

By the time I reach the next town, I am no longer angry with him. Just sad. He is young and still a fan of gestures. He may yet learn not to be so cavalier with Death. Perhaps because I am a more experienced suicidal, I understand there is a decorum to be respected, if one does not wish to be misunderstood.

Postcard Fourteen: Meteor Crater

They sell tickets to see it. Like going to a theater just to see the coming attractions. Questions haunt me as I drive away:

Could they see it coming, the mammoths, the camels and ground sloths of Arizona 50,000 years ago? Did they know the end had arrived? Will I?

Or has it already happened? Am I living in the shockwave still, holding on for the blissful incineration that releases us all?

Postcard Fifteen: Trickster

Among the intermittent sage, a coyote. Reminding me of our shared code, the same no matter the culture, this need for jokes along the way.

Postcard Sixteen: Roadkill

There is a recipe waiting for me in my email inbox, for a dish called "Million Dollar Pork Chops." I don't have that kind of money.

Day 10: Gallop, NM to Oklahoma City

Postcard Seventeen: Where I Drove and What I Drove For

Over the last two years, I've driven on some of the most amazing roads New Mexico, Colorado, Utah, and Arizona have to offer. Views of such staggering beauty that tears are the only appropriate tribute. For which, I am grateful.

I re-enter Oklahoma, reflection heavy. Last year was about healing; this year seems to be about understanding that healing. Understanding that these trips have morphed into migration. Understanding that I am most at peace, most happy driving on these roads, taking in these views and the perspectives they are gracious enough to lend. And that in spite of years of suffering and loneliness, in spite of the consuming darkness of depression, I find, with an eternal surprise, that I like being alone. There is one person I would exchange this shocked peace in return for company and partnership. But she lives in the west, and I have not made it that far. One of these years, I will reach her. But not yet. That is not the point of this trip.

There are still more roads, more views to come. Of such staggering beauty that tears are the only appropriate tribute. For which, I am grateful. Tolkien said it well. Not all who wander are lost. I have understood this for a good while. But now, I think I understand the other side of that coin. Those who don't, very well may be.

Paradigm Shift

"there is a crack in everything . . ."
                                    Leonard Cohen

The phrase contains a strong retrospective odor
of the obvious. A fish crawls out onto land
underneath a churning Devonian sky
and nothing will ever be the same.

Often it will ooze from underneath
the rubble of catastrophe. A dead Archduke,
the *Enola Gay*, Columbine.
And nothing will ever be the same.

But sometimes, it's subtle and quietly personal.
The soundless snap of a piece,
finally fitting into place.

The problem with healing
is that we use as the standard
the person we were before,
so often fail to see when it happens.

Like all paradigm shifts,
it can only be felt after the fact,
the unacknowledged moment of its arrival,
the grain itself gifted with the
spectral whimsey of a Tooth Fairy,
becomes blended into a sandscape of past.

There is just a day when you wake up
into calm realization, know with the
innateness of breath that you will never be whole again,
but also that you never were to begin with.

The vessel has always been cracked.
But now you know to marvel at the gift of that,
the perpetual pouring in it allows,
of which you will never be full.
And nothing will ever be the same.

Rarified Air

I have never understood the phrase "hopeless romantic."
A romantic is never hopeless.
Rather, they are *consumed* by Hope;
often, perhaps, to their own, foolish detriment,
but they are consumed by it nonetheless.

Or, if it be insisted they are indeed hopeless,
they are hopeless the way a mountaineer,
embraced by elevated view, seems hopeless
to the safe and comfortable below,
protected against the cold
by their modest fires, contained within homes
of thoughtless brick or tranquil stone.

Getting a Dog

I've been meaning to for a while,
ever since the divorce,
the removal of an ex-wife "cat person"
affording me a re-start on who I want to be.
But other than knowing with marrow-ingrained
sureness that I do not want another cat,
I have found it hard to proceed, uncertain,
as I set out into this redefined life,
what would be best, what it is I am looking for.

I am not unmindful of the symbolism of getting a puppy.
The boundless enthusiasm offering a return to youth.
A lightening of decades-collected weight,
erasing—or at the very least,
energetically smudging—the years of before.
Within each head tilt and playful yip
the *tabula rasa* of an innocent hedonism.
The look in its eyes that tells me everything is now ok,
that the weight and the before do not matter.

But then again, a rescue dog may be more apt.
A dog that has been through some shit,
carries its own scars with a grace I will then try to model.
There will be initial uncertainty, delayed trust,
but we will gradually settle into a new shared routine,
learn the limits of our interest in play,
find that perfect boundary between moments of silliness and of rest.
And in its eyes, instead of that Panglossian enthusiasm,
the simple promise of understanding,
of far more value, at this stage of the journey,
than the ceaseless licking of my face.

Not Lonely Enough

The issue clarified while watching, of all things,
a football game. The former player/analyst
making an off-hand comment
about the difference between pain and soreness.
Pain, he explained, is crippling;
soreness one can work through.

Maybe I am no longer drowning,
have learned the gift of flipper and blowhole.
Life rafts have certainly been offered,
ones for unexamined reasons I have chosen not to grab.
Perhaps I have fallen in love with the waves,
their tantalizing buoyancy, instead and have settled
into the comfortable solitude they offer.

Soreness does not mean healed.
There will be days the despair returns,
but perhaps it will do so as an old movie I've seen too many times
or as a nagging ankle injury that presages rain.

Like diesel exhaust from a passing truck
that for a moment—and for a moment only—
overwhelms the smell of morning woodsmoke
wafting from a neighbor's house,
the echo of pain will then settle back
into a truth un-heralded:

no longer the pain of loneliness,
but the symbolism of soreness,
a sighing celebration that I was never lonely enough.

Message in a Bottle

Perhaps the biggest obstacle to the end of loneliness
is not my balding spot,
nor the ever-greying that encircles it,
a frustrating follicle flanking maneuver
reconsidered and then abandoned;

It is not the twenty plus pounds that has clung to me
these last decades like pet hair on a well-used, slightly-sagging couch,
regardless of the efforts I take or don't take
to lose it;

And it is not the chimerical assemblage
of occasional monies I call a bank account;
nor is it the somewhere between susurrus and staccato snoring
I would serenade you with
(if I am lucky enough to get that far).

The biggest issue may be one of bedroom temperature
(if I am lucky enough to get that far).
I tend to keep mine cold as a meat locker.
So, unless my next life partner is a penguin or a side of beef,
I may be doomed to an endless succession of solitary nights.

But in mitigation (and hopeful invitation),
I offer the pet name my ex-wife gave me
back when we did stuff like give each other pet names:
On cold winter nights, she called me The Furnace.

On mornings like this one,
I like to think of you lying next to me.
(Whoever you are; wherever you may be.)
We could defy the outside cold,
press each into the other,
allow my warmth to be our warmth,
and hear with wonder the undulating thunder,
the rhythm of patterned rain drops
on this promising pleasantly-cool April morning,
then perhaps fall back into that liminal sleep space,
and dream a cold world away.

Left at the Trailhead

Father's Day, 2023.
Gloss Mountain State Park,
Oklahoma

It would be easy today
to let bitterness consume,
to focus on what has been stolen,
but the ascent was already arduous enough;
I should not carry such added weight.

With only the cloudless heat
to scour with healing burn,
with only a few thermalled
turkey vultures for companions,
atop appropriately named Cathedral Mountain,
absorbing its varied perspectives,
clutching a thirty-five-year-old walking stick
of Connecticut elm,
most of that bitterness fades away.
And for that, I am thankful.

It will still be there,
waiting to be re-collected,
on the way back.

Yet Another Landing Poem

"what matters most is how well you
walk through the fire."
Charles Bukowski

For years, I have felt the lack of a balcony, the apartment appendage where I would greet yet another morning with coffee. Usually I'd read some poetry, then return to the isolation inside and write my own, but there is no balcony where I live now. Just a cramped landing, barely big enough for one. Unlike a balcony, a landing cannot be shared. There is no room for a round bistro table that would hold our glasses of wine, the dinner I would cook. There is only room here for a single folding metal chair I found in the garage, rescued long ago by someone else from some elementary school or church basement, previous witness to earnest child performances, perhaps, or circular tales of recovery. On this weathered and rusty chair, within the confines of my not-balcony landing, I feel more Bukowski than Whitman.

Over these last handful of years, I have found restoration, but have also discovered that it does not last. It fades like a memory of fog. The sting of pain and loss linger in echo and shimmer. Bukowski said that what matters most is how well you walk through the fire. The problem with that is the suggestion of progression his verb choice hints at. I have long looked for an end zone, for a finish line, for the place where the fire stops and the burns start to heal.

But healing is not linear. The things that heal us must be returned to with a predictable regularity. Their potency is not permanent. And so maybe this landing is part of a cycle, a node in between balconies, the one that I've glorified by memory and the one whose vistas I have yet to obscure through routine. Or maybe the landing is a stop along a migration, a base camp of solitude, a necessary ground zero unfettered by rows of balconies alongside, rows of balconies across the way, their various privacies intruding into each other.

I do not know. What I *do* know is the Mississippi kites have returned, granting me an unexpected joy I could only witness from this landing. I once wrote a poem about their absence. I do not think I will write one (beyond this brief mention) about their return. Instead, I'm going to watch them hover and soar, while I sit with a cup of coffee on my landing, greeting the inconclusive balm of yet another morning.

My Other Son

I have not written many poems
about my youngest son.
Most of my son poems focus on my oldest,
whose mental landscape I share and understand,
and because this is true, of whom I worry.

Even when he was a child,
and I saw him every day, I did not worry
much about my youngest.
When we would go swimming,
he would ask me to pick him up,
launch-throw him from the firm footing
of the low end into the deeper water.
He, submerged, would break the water line
with a thumb-topped hand
letting me know he was ok,
that he would soon ask me to do it again.

I had to negotiate with a then prefix-free wife
to name him Emerson, a name to which she agreed
only after her crazy psychic friend gave a womb reading
declaring the unborn child already an "old soul."

So maybe that was why I was caught off-guard
by his reaction to a divorce everyone must have seen coming.
I assumed his placidity would be untouched,
that his precocious understanding of the world
would keep his heart whole, that the serenity
of an old soul could not be touched by something so mundane.
What was one more divorce to the world?

I did not fully reckon on that other, smaller world,
the one that was his; miscalculated
the fragility of a hidden youthful heart,
(of which I of all people should have known),
focused, as is often the way in such situations,
on my own health.

I thought an old soul would understand that.
I hoped an old soul would understand that.
I wanted to believe in the cacklings of a mad psychic.
I misunderstood the pool metaphor, if,
in fact, metaphor it was.

We share no firm footing now,
only the sound-distortion of full submersion,
in which the absence of a thumbs-up is deafening.
That I was acting in the best interests
of everyone involved seemed blinding true.
And it was.
Blind.
And yet true.

But that does not change the fact
that I have not written many poems
about my youngest son.

Proverb

The secret to catching something
is not to place your hand
where the object is,
but where it is going to be

The Comic

When you understand that someone
        else can tell a joke,
that you can let their anecdote
        breathe like a glass of fine Cabernet,
that you do not need to add a joke
        of your own to the strand,
that this is no place for one-upmanship,
that your time came before and will,
        perhaps, come again later,

you will finally understand the point
        and the value of humor.
It is then, and only then, that you can call
        yourself the comic.

Shaggy Dog

The comic has learned something funny. He has long been a fan, a fluent practitioner of the shaggy dog joke. He may, in fact, be a maestro, for he once told one that lasted 35 minutes and at no point during the telling was the attention of his audience anything other than spellbound. A style of joke that expands and contracts time, that meanders in the telling, doubling-back on itself, finding dead end after dead end. In fact, in some tellings it is *all* dead ends. There are no blueprints, no codified rules, no two tellings are ever the same. A joke that is all about the journey, a joke to which we already know the punchline (even if we don't), and which we always find disappointing, usually delightfully so.

Those are the jokes the comic liked best to tell. He had one about a stuttering salesman, one about a moth visiting a podiatrist, one that ends with the punchline, "I'd love to tell you, but you're not a monk."

But now, he has learned something funny. Since he has let his hair grow long, longer than he ever imagined (except that damn bald spot. Nothing seems to cover that damned bald spot, stubbornly claiming its small patch of scalp since the mid-90s—and since the comic hopes his work will remain long—longer even that his hair—after he has gone, he should emphasize he means the 1990s), he finds hair, long hair, all over his apartment. He finds it gathered in floor-corners, in tub drains and sinks; he finds it stubbornly clinging to his purple couch. It is everywhere. At first, he blamed his dog, but then remembered he does not have a dog. And *that's* when he learned something funny. *He* is the dog. A shaggy one. The comic, at long last, has become the kind of joke he likes to tell. A blending that makes him smile, re-focusing his attention where he has always known (but somehow never suspected) it needed to be.

To the Reader

Sometimes, when I'm out in public,
running errands, a quick run to Walmart
or the post office,
or on vacation, meandering
through western states on a migration
dedicated to renewal
        (for it is only the west, where
        the horizon lives, that heals),
wounds becoming scabs
becoming scars
becoming part of the ever-changing
cartography of the self,

I'll pass a couple.
The man will say something funny
and the woman, who is always beautiful,
will laugh.

In these moments, I must admit,
I still feel the sting,
however muted,
of having no one to tell my jokes to.

So, I will tell them to you
in the hopes you, like the always-beautiful
woman, will laugh.

And if you don't find them funny,
then we will both be spared
the awkward silence that follows.

Prophetic

On the middle urinal,
a hand-written sign that reads:
                    "Out of Order"
With an arrow pointing down like this:
                    ↓

I find the declaration premature.
I am not that old yet.

Suicidal

"The way is to the destructive element submit yourself,
and with the exertions of your hands and feet in the water
make the deep, deep sea keep you up."

Joseph Conrad, *Lord Jim*

Some days, some months, some years
it feels like the world does not want me in it,
is actively, aggressively, opposed to the idea.
And for the most part, I have given up trying to convince it
otherwise.
Like water, pain finds its level.
And as Stein says in *Lord Jim*, our job is simply to stay afloat.
I have no doubt the advice is meant to be helpful.

I don't want to stay here;
tried once already to leave,
and yet here I continue to linger.
I do not wish to dog-paddle through
the days, the months, the years.
I wish to grab hold of some neutral, unbiased
weight and let it drag me down into the void.

But instead, I find myself packing the car once again,
heading out on another ritualized migration.
I don't know why I keep taking these long, winding road trips.
I don't know why I always head west.
I don't know what it is I'm hoping to find.
And I don't understand why I haven't found it yet.

I use the word the way a drinker might use "alcoholic,"
because I don't think the urge ever fully goes away.
Maybe with medication,
but I do not wish a medicated life.

So, instead, I will tie myself to the mast.
Sometimes I will jam wax in my ears.
And sometimes I won't,
braving the full-throated roar of the Sirens
in the faint hope I'll catch a lyric that makes sense,
one that explains the days, the months, and the years.

Death Valley

I killed a man this morning.

Perhaps I could have taken him with me up Golden Canyon,
have him sit beside me in Red Cathedral,
but the weight would have been too great,
and it is just the right kind of silent here without him.

I had intended to look down at him from the height of Zabriski
Point,
but there were too many other vistas to distract me,
heat shimmering up from the basin floor
whispering its cauterized blessing.

I took Gower's Gulch back down,
passing abandoned borax mines
with their reminders that the past is poison;
wandered through the raised earth-scar of badlands
embraced by the solace of insignificance,
folds of rock in verity declaration
that a desolate beauty is beauty still.

There was no sign of him back at the trail head.
Perhaps the crows found him.
Perhaps he wandered off into a different story.

I do not know.
All I do know is that he is gone.
It was long overdue,
and I don't think anyone will miss him.

Reading *Practical Gods* While Visiting National Parks

For Carl Dennis

"Be brave, Soul," I want to say to encourage it.
"Your student, however slow, is willing"

As you say in your opening poem about Hermes, the way down from there to here may still be open, so ever since a dear poet friend introduced me to your work with a spontaneous and emotional reading of "The God Who Loves You," I've been on the lookout for where your practical gods perch, watching us with the trepidation of estranged but still worried parents or of long-disconnected friends.

And now, Carl, I think I found them. While there is nothing practical about the searing heat of Death Valley's basin, nor in the height and girth of the sequoia, the point of these lands, and of the others like them, a panoply of wisdom in their own right, is the same. This assemblage of Majestics, standing on their own Olympus, christened Angel's Landing or Half Dome, remind us to stay in the moment, to not chase the life we could have had at the expense of the one we witness.

Visiting these gods is a reminder that there is so much beauty in the world, and that more often than we realize but not as often as we should, we participate in it. Standing on top of Moro's Rock, I hear these practical gods whisper to me, Carl, and because I do, I tell my old bones, my fallow muscles, that I am not out of breath; I am only just now learning to breathe. Which is all the god who loves us could ever wish for.

Share the Road

I have driven on some great roads. Breath-taking, majestic, inspiring roads. Roads that break me down, reassemble with an awesome, tear-laden joy. The closest I'm ever likely to come to an apprehension of God, this sense of something larger, something that while it may not love me, not in the way robed proselytizers promise from Sunday pulpits, does acknowledge my right to be there unacknowledged.

State highway 82 in Colorado, for example, which brings you up into the Rockies, crosses the Continental Divide at Independence Pass. Over 12,000 feet above sea level, one of the highest paved roads in the country. Even in June you are not guaranteed a snowless pass. Cut into the side of the mountains, death-fall inches away, separated by what seem far-too-flimsy guardrails, the road shows you in indisputable terms your own mortality and then comforts you with the reminder of how insignificant that fact is.

There is a road in Utah that cuts through the Manti-La Sal National Forest, connecting the small towns of Fairview in the west with Huntington in the east. Lightly-traveled, staggeringly beautiful and despite its remoteness, never out-of-the-way. On an atlas, it is barely a palpable squiggle that will take you up over 9,000 ft, grace you with alpine lake after alpine lake, offer cold creeks within which you may anoint your penitent feet, then bring you windingly down through majestic canyonland. While Independence Pass whispers your meaningless and beautiful death, it is Life, equally meaningless and beautiful, that is celebrated here.

There are other roads as well. U.S. 191 in Utah; U.S. 89 in Arizona, connecting Paige to Flagstaff; Emory Pass in New Mexico; state highway 178 through the southern Sierra in California; the birthing of U.S. 82 into the Lincoln Forest.

One day, when I find you, I will ask if you would like to see them, if you wish to share these vistas with me. And if it seems appropriate (for sometimes shared silence is what the scene will demand), I will share with you the thoughts these vistas provoke. Perhaps you will do the same.

Serene But Not Well

It is hard not to see this life as a failure.
It bears none of the external markers of success.
It would be easy for someone outside to see
the shotgun one-bedroom garage apartment,
the ten-year-old used car, the one humble meal
a day, the barren cracked-leather wallet,
and conclude these are the trappings
of a could-have-been, of a never-was-nor-will-be.
The closest indicator of a success I can point to
is owning fourteen pairs of Chuck Taylor's.

It is hard not to see this life as a failure.
I understand, and for the most part agree, but
I would put in a few words of mitigation; would
cite an outsider's blissful ignorance of the swells and summits
of bipolar madness, the plummet of depression that
hollows you out with Life; the manic burst of heights,
body tingling in eruption of the Same.
Would cite the carefully-crafted solitude
I simultaneously bemoan and protect, a confused
Cerberus growling against bribe dreams of flesh.

Yes, it is hard not to see this life as a failure.
But, the birds, the books, wind and rivers,
steaming coffee on cool November mornings.
Some days—more than I tend to admit; less
than I truly need—the serenity of these
is a kind of enough. If not markers of a type of success,
at the very least, a kind of failure uniquely, beautifully,
my own, licking me with the abrasive love
of a mother cat's tongue.

Four Years Later

"For who would bear the whips and scorns of time"
Hamlet III, i

You wonder if you've used the time wisely,
whether you've contributed,
in this stolen time,
anything more than carbon dioxide.

You use the word "suicidal,"
with the same self-referential
significance of alcoholics,
for you know that while clouds part,
they also return.

Sometimes people congratulate you,
mistaking your inefficiency for a change of heart,
unable to acknowledge your full commitment
to an idea not dreamt of in their philosophy.

Sometimes you sit with Hope—
cradling it like a newborn,
knowing the world it will grow into,
knowing that world has no place for it—
and think you are four years behind schedule.

Sometimes you think of the things
you've been able to see and do in the last four years:
a game of catch with poets,
an elk astride the Continental Divide,
alpine lakes in Nevada,
a Petrified Forest,
an old friend's first novel,

think of the things you still hope to see
in the time left before someone in Accounting
notices the ledger is off:
Angel's Landing in Zion,
the Yellowstone again,

the redwoods reached, finally, in the West
(although you know now there will be
no one standing next to them)

And sometimes you can speak, Lazarus-like,
to friends of their trauma and tragedy,
offer a unique perspective they do not have
(nor would you want them to).

You wonder if a life of shadow and echo
is still a life, wonder what will happen
if the shimmer never ceases shimmering,
never coalesces into form, wonder
if a desert ceases to be one if you accept the oasis
was always a mirage, or does that make the aridity,
the heat, more unbearable still?

And sometimes you will remember
that endorheic lakes are
refilled by occasional rainfall.

If, on anniversaries like this,
you want to buy a birthday cake,
treat this day like a second birth,
do this for yourself.

But do not bother with candles.
You are beyond the relevance of wishes now,
and the darkness of a blown-out light
comes soon enough.

Ripple

"If I knew the way, I would take you home."
The Grateful Dead

It's been more than a week since I found out. I've waited that long to write this because I was afraid. Not of emotions set loose but a fear I would have nothing to say. Auden has already stopped the clocks, cut off the telephone. How could I say more? And Jerry Garcia proclaims that path is for your steps alone, that I cannot follow. What wisdom or poignancy can I add to that? I do find myself hoping where you are now has endless fields of flowers from which you may choose one to adorn your hair, remaining in memory ways you could not in life. But otherwise, I find myself, carved out by earlier goodbyes, devoid of an appropriate vocabulary. To say something like I am just now learning there is a dark darker than dark would be performative and trite; to speak of a blackness scripted with the new permanence of Never would simply make my friends worry.

Of course, Garcia also gives up on words by the end of the song, choosing instead the ancient harmony of vocalization, and thinking of you this morning, listening to the patterned wetness, the serene grumbling of thunderstorm, I can appreciate why. Lack of words does not signal apathy or defeat or despair or hopelessness; it is, rather, a grounding upon a foundation more intrinsic than language, made of the primal material of mountains, gales, and waves, stretching forward and backward with a timelessness of which we were mere echo and shadow, revered forgotten pieces of a once and future whole.

The World Without Us

The park across the street this March morning
is stuck in the stasis of inhale,
its white frosted grass matching
the precocious bloom of cottonwood.
You have been gone a few months now.

I watch my neighbor pack his truck and go inside.
A few moments later, he starts his truck
from the warm safety of his living room.

There is so much we can do
without ourselves now:
Starting a truck,
keeping an inventory,
raining fire on the world,
even the writing of a love letter;
all, training the world for our absence.

A helpful reminder how little waits on me.
How the world will continue—
more or less the same—once I am gone.
You have been gone a few months now.
And the park across the street this March morning
is stuck in the stasis of inhale.

Summer Break

It is now the season of the clichéd envy
teachers deal with every year,
the ignorant masses chiding our summers "off,"
telling us how nice it must be.

(They always neglect the corollary:
that paychecks also take the summer off.)

What the break means for me
is that I get an uninterrupted series
of mornings with coffee and poetry
on my landing.

And at this point,
that's all the happiness I find.
And many mornings,
all the happiness I need.

No expensive vacations,
no elaborate projects
for the yard. No begrudged
visits to family. No water parks
or beaches.

Just coffee and poetry on my landing.
That's it. Just coffee and poetry
on my landing. With just the birds
for company. And thoughts.
Not all of which are about you.

Transhumance

When the shepherds and the tenders of cattle
leave for the highlands each summer,
they unknowingly take me with them.
Mountains call, and I respond,
car laden with jerky and granola,
hiking boots, mud-caked and tattered,
walking stick of Connecticut elm,
four-decade veteran of alpine wood
and sun-blazoned sandstone.

The great crime of the circle
seems to be that it is not a line.
A gaze that is not rigid and future-focused
is too often mislabeled stagnation.
Draped in false allusions to hamster wheels
or the opprobrium of a perceived
ennui, it is easy to forget migration
is a word that excludes only the unimaginative,
that it is not livestock alone that needs be led to graze.

To return from whence you started,
dusted with the patina of journey
is not failure. Trees do not tell
their stories in lines; nor should we.
Lost in the din of chanted canticles
to myths of progress, lost in the math
that measures distance in miles,
is an inner core of self that is fed
by the cyclical ebb and flow
of a leaving and of a return.

Rest Area

"Don't let the past remind us
of what we are not now."
                        Stephen Stills

Unaccountable whim pulls me into the rest area off I-40 in
panhandled Texas. I have long avoided this place, fearful of the
ghosts there.

We stopped here once before, in the long ago of family road trips,
before divorce and the ripple-effect of divorce claimed them.

Every time I've passed since, the sting of phantom pain, the golden
sheen of diorama: How both sons were equally fascinated and
terrified by ubiquitous "Watch for rattlesnakes" signs, yet rushed up
the earth-bermed facilities anyway to enjoy the seemingly endless red
rock vistas and the possibility of pronghorn.

Now, with the unsteady legs of one long at sea, I stumble into
certainties:
that the past lingers within a gilded fog of its own making,
that without a vital vigilance, we create our own demons.

The fact of paths I distinctly remember them running up
is contradicted by signs telling visitors they may not climb on the hill.

The fact of the elevated platform from which they gazed into their
uncertain horizons
is belied by its absence.

And there are exactly zero signs mentioning rattlesnakes.

There is only endless red rock vistas and the possibility of pronghorn.

All Out of Road

I heard once that the Pacific
has no memory, but now, my feet
bathed in its cold northern waters, I find
that that is not the same promise as Lethe's.
Sometimes, the you that few others knew
wove a story about the two of us sitting
on shore rock, our feet washed by these waves.
But you are not here now and this is no story.
In the gap between the promise of then
and the absence of now, I know this ocean
rinsing my feet rinsed yours as well,
and that, I suppose, will have to do.
In the several lonely harbors I stopped at earlier,
the waves pounded the shore in formless rage,
but here they lap with the hush of susurrus lullaby.
Tomorrow, I'll go see the redwoods.
I'm told they're beautiful.
I'm sure they are.

Experto Credite

Katabasis

*"Experto credite"**
The Aeneid

Know that I have been here before,
and can show you the way,
show you how to accept the catadromous path
which led you into this great darkness,
this vastness of hyperplasic despair.

While the priests above pray to gods
they do not understand;
while frail kings finger their toys of war,
dreaming pyrolatrous Armageddon,
their navels crusted with the dried seed of
their once-prideful youth;
while wise men abdicate the trappings of wisdom,
retreating into the safety of silence and solitude;
know that I have been here before.

Know also that you are not the first to stumble
into this dark,
wayward youth in search of monsters
and of beds to hide them under.
Odysseus, Aeneas, Dante,
all floundered within to find
some way out again,
discovering not what was wanted,
but what was ordained by
the casual acrostic prognostication of
a palimpsest prophecy.

And know that you will not be the last, either.
I will wait for the others as I waited for you.

Tour guide of the kaleidoscopic,
        curator of boxes long since emptied of
        sea glass and bric-a-brac,
I sometimes like to pretend I am Orpheus,

practice the impossible task
of not looking back

(and like Vonnegut, I will always love Lot's wife
for understanding the essential salve of doing so)

for if I am not followed, whom will I follow in turn?
A chain that is not chain is just a ring.

Yes, I know you can hear the drum thunder from above,
       and the clarion call;
but do you not also hear the wood-creak of the settling house,
       the trilling of water over stone,
       the fanfare silence of carved rock under domes of heat,
       and the storytelling of rain clouds?

Listen into and beyond the static anthem from above.
Breathe deep,
fill your lungs with petrichor air,
and know that I have been here before.
And I will show you the way.

*Trust one who has gone through it.

Acknowledgments

With gratitude to the editors of the journals and anthologies where the following poems first appeared:

Behind the Rain: An Anthology of Oklahoma Poetry: "Murrah" (also winner of 2024 ROMP Oklahoma Poem Award), "In a Children's Museum" and "After Mt. Moriah."

The Mackinaw: A Journal of Prose Poetry: "End of Days," "Shaggy Dog," "The Old Men at Walmart" (nominated for Best of the Net, 2025) and "Unrequited."

Oklahoma Today: "Envy" and "I Heard a Woodpecker in Oklahoma City."

Windward Review: "Age of Heroes" and "Reading Galway Kinnell's *When One Has Lived a Long Time Alone.*"

Emerge Magazine: "Transhumance" (winner of 2025 Woody Barlow Poetry Contest).

Additionally, the poems, "On T.V." and "Thoughts of a Useful Idiot: A Prose Persona Poem" first appeared in *Butterflies in Gaza: A World Anthology of Poems on Peace* (Nsemia Publishing).

I'd also like to express my profound appreciation for Paul Bowers and Turning Plow Press, not just for his too-overlooked contribution to giving Oklahoma writers a bigger footprint, but for his constant support and encouragement of my work. Your continual words of praise mystify me, but they are deeply cherished.

About the Author

Paul Juhasz is a Pushcart and Best of the Net nominated author of five books: *Fulfillment: Diary of a Warehouse Picker*, a mock journal chronicling his seven-month term as a picker at an Amazon Fulfillment Center; *As If Place Matters*, a collection of short fiction; and three collections of poetry: *Ronin: Mostly Prose Poems*, a finalist for the 2022 Oklahoma Book Award, *The Inner Life of Comics*, and *The Fires of Heraclitus*, a finalist for the 2025 Oklahoma Book Award. He served as curator and coordinator of the Woody Guthrie Poets from 2020-2024, and currently lives in Oklahoma City.